The Secret of Couture Sewing
by Roxane

McGRAW-HILL BOOK COMPANY
New York St. Louis San Francisco Düsseldorf
London Mexico Sydney Toronto

Contents

To my three sons_____

Introduction

CONSIDER the difference between a TV Dinner and a full-course gourmet meal...between an abbreviated news story and a full-length book...between a two-line children's song and a magnificent symphony. If you can appreciate these contrasts, you'll understand the comparison between what I call sew-and-go fashions and true designer originals.

With today's burgeoning home-sewing market, it's easy to recognize the appeal of "instant fashion." Wonderful fabrics are readily available...and hundreds of easy-to-sew patterns are waiting to tempt you. The idea of selecting a fabric, cutting it out and whipping up a new costume in a matter of hours is almost irresistible.

My point is this: how attractive will that new outfit be? And equally important, how long will it last? Will you have to admit in apology, "I made it myself"? The purpose of this book is to have you explain, with *pride,* "I sewed it," when your friends are begging you for the name of your secret fashion source!

Every do-it-yourself dressmaker knows the basics of sewing. If she didn't learn when her machine was purchased, or in school, the quick-way instructions are often listed right in the pattern envelope. Certainly, you must know the basics before you go one step further. This book, however, deals with the *specifics*—the technical secrets that take you out of the world of the amateur and into the marvelously satisfying realm of couture design.

These methods cannot be called "sew-and-go." They require patience, patience, patience. You will learn *why* you are doing certain things as well as *how.* You will concentrate on shape, inner construction, proper fit and simplicity of line. You will grasp the fundamentals of good basic design, the keynote for infinite chic variations.

Most of all, you'll be able to create custom fash-

ions for yourself and your lucky "customers" that will spell designer flair. As it is in cooking, in music, in literature—indeed in any art form, and couturier sewing is an art form—there is a wrong way and a right way of going about a creative project. This book will show you the tried and true, *professionally* right methods for sewing your own couture wardrobe.

—Roxane

Partners in Fashion: Your Equipment

I

Would you believe that little more than one hundred twenty years ago, women were still sewing all their clothes by hand? Even after Isaac Singer invented his sewing machine in 1851, making your clothes at home was never as chic as having a "little dressmaker." Today, however, the tables are turned and "the little old dressmaker–*you*" can capture compliments and enjoy the creativity of doing-it-yourself. This, of course, is only possible if you own a latter-day version of Mr. Singer's lifesaver.

Your machine is indeed a best friend and will always perform loyally if you treat it properly. Study the manual carefully for instructions on the care and feeding (yes, oil) of your machine. Be sure the operation is smooth and quiet, the stitches are even and, most important, that the machine is threaded properly.

Learn to regulate your machine so that the tension is correct–this produces an even stitch without pulling either the top or bottom layer of the fabric. Experiment by cutting a strip of fabric on the length grain and running a few rows of stitching before you start on your actual sewing. According to the type of fabric and how tightly you want to stitch, the manual will give directions for adjusting to:

- REGULATION STITCH: *12 to 16 stitches per inch*
- EASE STITCH: *10 stitches per inch*
- REINFORCING STITCH: *20 stitches per inch*

Stitches should always be secured at the beginning and end of a seam. You can achieve this by lifting the pressure foot slightly and shifting the fabric back and forth for ½". Another method for securing

THE SEWING MACHINE: A FAITHFUL FRIEND

[1]

the stitch is to leave about 4″ of thread at either end and tie the ends by hand.

Guide your fabric on the sewing line by holding it with one hand behind the pressure foot and one in front of it. Since the sewing line is clearly indicated on the fabric, if you have followed construction marking directions carefully, you will not have to follow the guide lines on the machine. Just sew on the basting lines that will be removed prior to pressing the seam.

Always choose the proper thread and needles for the fabric you are working on. When sewing knit fabrics, for example, it is advisable to use a polyester-blend thread that stretches with the knit. Working on synthetic leather fabric may require a heavier needle. Attention to these small details will bring about better results.

CUTTING, SEWING AIDS MAKE THE JOB GO SMOOTHLY

a cutting board with dots or square
    markings to indicate grain
dressmaker's tracing paper
chalk pencils
tracing wheel
satin pins—leave no mark in delicate fabrics
tailor's push pins
thimble
needles (several sizes)
mercerized thread and synthetic thread
    for synthetic fabrics and knits
bent-handle shears
trimming shears
tape measure
yardstick
transparent ruler
triangular ruler to indicate perfect
    bias grain
a steam iron
an ironing board
a sleeve board
a ham-shaped cushion for curved seams
    and darts
a pounding block to flatten woolens when
    they are steamed
a wool press cloth; a heavy muslin cloth
skirt marker for lengths

How to Be Size-Wise

ONE of the most important reasons for sewing your own clothes is to *achieve perfect fit.* This, however, is sometimes difficult when you are both model and tailor. A good way of by-passing this problem is to use a dress form, preferably one that's exactly your shape, size and proportions (see figure 1). Unfortunately, since time has a way of playing games with one's figure, even a specially made form can vary from the actual measurements of your body. Every few months check your measurements against those of the form; if there is a deviation, here's a foolproof way to alter that "dummy."

• Buy a dress form as close to your own measurements as possible (but not larger than you are).

• Cut a high-necked, sleeveless "body" from medium-weight unbleached muslin, using a basic pattern with a center seam, side seams and a seam from the shoulder over the bust. The "body" should be as long as the dress form. Baste seams together, leaving center back seam partially open.

• Fit this muslin on yourself with the seams on the outside. Wear a long bra and girdle so that muslin can be fitted *tightly and smoothly* to your body, without wrinkles.

• Make whatever adjustments and corrections are necessary. Re-baste with small stitches and try it on again, this time with seams pressed open lightly and worn *inside.* If muslin fits smoothly on your body, stitch all seams, including back seam, and press open.

• Place this muslin over your dress form and stuff it firmly with cotton or thin sheets of urethane foam. The form will now conform to your exact shape and enable you to do all fittings easily.

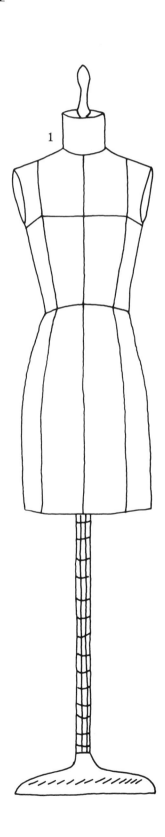

1

SIZE FORTY AND OVER CAN MEAN QUALITY

If you're over size 40, you can look as chic and well dressed as any size 14. There's no need to be discouraged—your clothes can be made as well as those of your small-sized counterpart. The trick is to select fabrics and designs that will be right for you.

Here are a few DON'TS:

DON'T choose large pattern prints.
DON'T choose heavy, bulky fabrics.
DON'T choose thin, clingy fabrics.
DON'T go haywire with fireman's red or screaming green.
DON'T choose patterns that are too "choppy."
DON'T overtrim.
DON'T fit your clothes so tightly that all the bulges show. Fit them with ease.
DON'T wear full skirts. A-line or straight will do more for you.
DON'T wear pants unless you wear a long tunic to cover the seat entirely.

Couture Tips

■ Remember, a seam center front or a front closing will minimize the width across the front. The front seam can be welted to give importance and act as detail.

■ A dress with a waistline will help if you do not have a large "roll" above it.

■ The system for making clothes for larger sizes is no different from making clothes for small sizes. Follow the same instructions.

■ Don't take short cuts—you'll be disappointed if your clothes don't come up to expectations.

■ Larger women should take extra care to see that they are fitted properly.

■ There are many large women who are extremely chic. It's not what you do, but how you do it.

■ Being well groomed will make your clothes look better—whatever your size!

SIZE-WISE GUIDE: FOR COMMERCIAL PATTERNS

MISSES' SIZES

	6	8	10	12	14	16	18
Bust	31	31½	32½	34	36	38	40
Waist	22	23	24	25½	27	29	31
Hips	33	34	35	36	37½	39½	41
Back waist (nape of neck to waist)	15¼	15½	15¾	16	16¼	16½	16¾

WOMEN'S SIZES

	20	40	42	44	46	48	50
Bust	42	44	46	48	50	52	54
Waist	34	36	38	40½	43	45½	48
Hips	44	46	48	50	52	54	56
Back waist (nape of neck to waist)	17	17¼	17½	17⅝	17¾	17⅞	18

JUNIOR SIZES

	5	7	9	11	13	15
Bust	30	31	32	33½	35	37
Waist	21½	22½	23½	24½	26	28
Hips	32	33	34	35½	37	39
Back waist (nape of neck to waist)	15	15¼	15½	15¾	16	16¼

PERSONAL MEASUREMENTS
(compare with pattern)

Bust ____________________

Waist ____________________

Hips ____________________

Back waist (nape of neck to waist) ____________________

Basically, a Designing Woman

III

ALL fashion emanates from basic design principles. Fashion doesn't change a basic design—*you* change a basic design to accommodate current fashion. Ironically, many so-called basic designs aren't basic at all. A basic pattern is one that adapts to all fashion trends and lends itself to many versions and variations of design.

Basic means...uncluttered lines, with as few seams as necessary to achieve a good shape. If fashion says "closer to the body," you nip the seams. If it says "looser fit," you let them out.

Basic means...simplicity in cut and fit.

Basic means...the garment lends itself to variations in trimming.

Basic means...you can cut through for additional seaming for shaping or as detail.

Basic means...you can now enter the heady heights of do-it-yourself design. Your pattern affords you the flexibility of originality.

Basic means...forever. There's no time limit on using a basic pattern—nor is there a limit for versatility. You can create fashions for sports, cocktails, evening.

Basic means...the joy of working on a dress you *know* will fit well.

For a complete wardrobe you need only two or three basic dress patterns, one or two coat designs, two skirts and your favorite pants pattern. Here it's what you do in the way of variations that will give you infinite selections. To work with these specifics is a primary rule of creating couturier clothes. Per-

[6]

fecting your basic patterns may take a little longer, but you'll enjoy so much improvement in the finished garment. Once you become accustomed to working this way you will actually find it easier. You'll never go back to making clothes the sew-and-go way.

These are the basic designs for wardrobe staples:

DRESS BASICS: a semi-fitted shift or princess line (on preceding page, see fig. 1); A-lined or flared, various seams (2, 3); a basic waistline dress (4);

THE FUNDAMENTALS

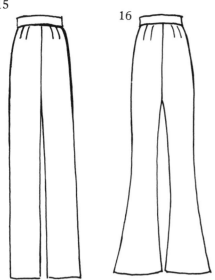

a shirtwaist dress in one piece or with cut-through waistline (5).

COAT BASICS: straight, semi-fitted (6); A-line, fitted and flared (7, 8); wrapped and belted (9).

SKIRT BASICS: flared (10); pleated (11); A-line (12); side-wrapped (13); front-buttoned (14).

PANTS BASICS: side or front closing (15); vary the width of the legs to match current fashion by widening or narrowing from the knee down (16).

The Patterns for Fashion

IV

LITERALLY hundreds of new patterns are introduced each season. The possibilities for fashion are, therefore, virtually unlimited. While this can be a bonanza for styling inspiration, it can also cause confusion. Keep in mind the importance of basic designs and rely on your imagination for variations, rather than depending too heavily on an intricately designed pattern which may not fit well, sew well and, ultimately, look well.

MAKE SURE THE SIZE IS RIGHT

Before selecting a pattern, you must be sure of your size. First take your own measurements carefully

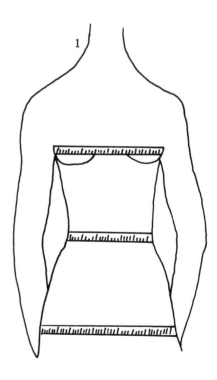

(1). Place a measuring tape around the fullest area of the bust; next measure your waistline and then the hip (usually at the fullest part, about 7″ down from the waistline). It's also important to check the length of the waist in back by measuring from the center of the large bone at the back of the neck to the waistline. Don't tighten the tape when taking measurements. Compare your own measurements with those on the chart in Chapter 2 and choose a size closest to your own. Remember, a small allowance for ease and comfort is always accounted for on all patterns. The actual measurements given on a pattern are *body* measurements.

▪ The sizes used in patterns in the back of this book are different from commercial patterns and approximately equivalent to the sizes of ready-to-wear clothes. Manufacturers, whether boutique or couture, employ a standard measurement chart supplied by the industry. Measurements may vary slightly, depending on the manufacturer; since some like to have their clothes fit very closely to the figure and others allow for ease. But basically they

do not change to any great degree. If you wear a size 10 in ready-to-wear, it would be safe to select a size 10 pattern.

SELECTING A SPECIFIC STYLE

Often, two or three sketches are included on each envelope showing the variations that can be made using the basic pattern and several changes, such as different sleeves or necklines, pants instead of a skirt. Each variation is marked View 1, 2, 3, etc., indicating that each unit of a pattern will include these markings so that you know which units to use for each design. (Each piece of the pattern is numbered and each number has a reference chart to tell you what it refers to.) Always study the pattern well before cutting to make sure you have the right pieces for your selection.

• Patterns will indicate necessary yardage. If the fabric you have in mind has a design which must be matched, or should be cut in one direction because of nap or shading, make sure you allow for additional yardage. A suggested layout for cutting is also included (2). It's always best to lay out the entire pattern on your underlining to utilize the fabric to best advantage, without waste. Never deviate from the grain line to save fabric—and, if possible, cut your fabric on the double. (In some cases, several pieces may require cutting from a single layer.)

• Don't throw away the pattern envelope—you'll be referring to it throughout the process of making your garment. If you find it unwieldy to stuff all the pattern pieces back in the original envelope, transfer all pieces to a 10″ x 14″ envelope, retaining the important front and back sections of the pattern envelope.

ALTERING YOUR PATTERN FOR CUSTOM FIT

All patterns require some alteration—even if fitting professional models. No one is 100 percent perfect and the measurements of every individual vary. Fit changes according to height, weight and bone structure; the measurements used in patterns are only an average for all figures of a general size.

▪ Many sewing books advise altering the actual pattern to adjust fit and measurements. This is a very technical study to try "out of hand" and in my opinion requires a great deal of experience. Even if all the measurements were adjusted to yours, perfect fit would still not be assured.

▪ The only way to achieve fitting perfection is to cut your pattern in unbleached muslin, sew it together very accurately and *then* do your fitting. This is the method used by couturiers every time they add a new model to their collections–even though they have the expertise to cut directly into a fabric, thereby saving time. They always make a muslin

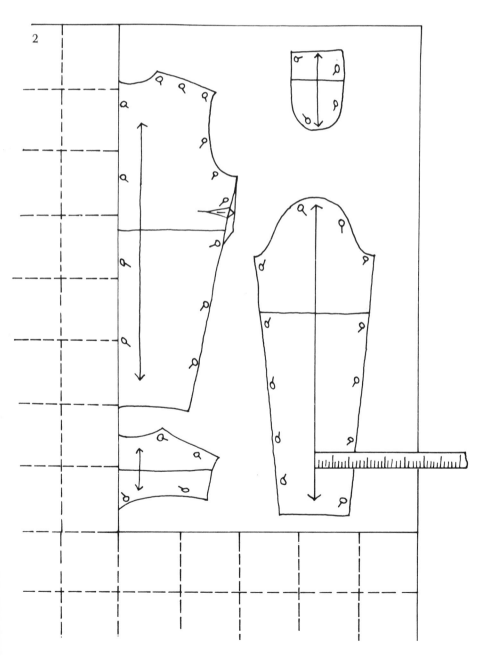

first to be sure the style they are creating will have proper shape and will lend itself to the seaming indicated by the pattern.

▪ Furthermore, making a muslin isn't a waste of time at all! Now you will have a permanent reference for use in part or whole whenever working on this particular basic design. A muslin can be a terrific money-saver as well—it eliminates the frustrating errors that could well occur when cutting directly into expensive fabrics. I can't emphasize enough this important step. As I mentioned before, there is only one way to proceed with couturier sewing: the correct way. Don't try to take short cuts. It's better to own one fine custom-made garment than three slapped-together sew-and-go items.

▪ For alterations on a muslin, mark them with red chalk so you won't be confused by the original construction markings. Then, take the muslin apart, press it carefully, and it's ready for use as a pattern. Although you may cut directly from the muslin, I suggest transferring the pattern onto hard or brown paper, making sure that all construction lines and symbols are accurately included, using tracing paper and a tracing wheel. This creates what is called a "template"—a pattern that becomes a permanent reference. In addition, it's much easier to mark your fabric using a hard paper pattern, since it doesn't shift or curl as much as muslin or the original tissue paper would.

In adjusting your pattern, the following seam-allowance guide should be considered:

▪ GARMENT SEAMS—*1 inch*

▪ SLEEVE SEAMS—*¾ inch*

▪ SHOULDER SEAMS—*⅝ inch*

▪ ARMHOLE—*⅝ inch*

▪ HEMS—*3 inches for dresses, 2½ inches for coats*
  (a wide hem helps your garment hang better)

▪ Even though your altered pattern is as close to perfect as possible, there may still be slight adjustments to make on your finished garment, since all fabrics react differently. Be patient and don't let that worry you. Meticulous attention to fit is the name of the couture-sewing game.

Figure Problems

V

AS noted several times before, there is no such thing as a pattern that will fit perfectly, without any alterations. The seams may have to be larger...or smaller; the length may have to be longer...or shorter; the sleeves may feel too tight ...the neckline may be too loose.

Since it's hard to anticipate in advance, cut your muslin according to directions, sew it accurately and then be prepared to make changes. Following are typical fitting problems with suggested corrections; in some instances, there is more than one approach to altering your muslin. You'll find that with the exception of a separation section on pants or shorts (which do require several adjustments to really fit properly), our concentration is on the bodice of a dress or, similarly, a blouse, suit jacket or coat "top." In these cases, the armholes, sleeves, darts, bust-line, neckline, etc., are details that can "throw off" the entire fit of your designer costume. On the other hand, most skirts can easily be adjusted as to length (via hemming) or width (via side seams) and require little detailed explanation.

WAIST

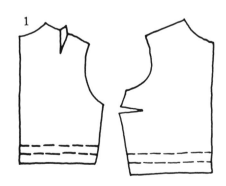

- SHORT-WAISTED *(front and/or back)* SOLUTION: you may be able to shorten the waist simply by taking in a ½" larger seam at the waistline (1). Try this first by pinning up the excess to see if such shortening works.

  Another method is to take up the necessary amount of slack via a tuck placed about 2" above the waistline of the pattern. Baste the tuck in place; then try on the waist again.

- LONG-WAISTED *(front and/or back)* SOLUTION: if your muslin is ½" (or less) too short for the long-waisted figure, it may be possible to simply take a ½" seam at the waistline instead of the allocated

[13]

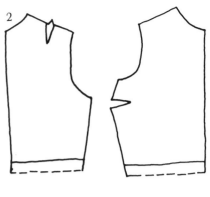

1″ (2). Rip out your muslin, reduce the seam allowance and try on again.

However, it may be necessary to cut a new muslin (or correct the original), allowing the necessary amount of inches via an extension about 2″ above the waistline. (Note: Patterns usually indicate a lengthening or shortening line; you may use their suggested line as a guide for making waistline adjustments, as described here.)

- LARGE WAISTLINE, FRONT ONLY (*indicated by side seam swinging toward the front of the garment, rather than hanging straight*) SOLUTION: if your waistline is evenly wide (both front and back), all you have to do is take a smaller seam on all four side edges of front and back bodice. For a large front waistline, however, you may have to add another inch of muslin to your pattern on each side of the front waist, tapering off to nothing at the underarm dart (3).

SHOULDERS

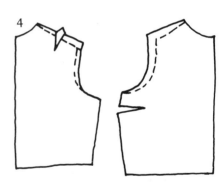

- NARROW SHOULDERS, SLOPING SHOULDERS SOLUTION: the correction may be as simple as taking a larger seam at the shoulder-part of the armhole and tapering back to original seam allowance at underarms. Or, if there is a dart included on the back shoulder line, increase it (4). If there is no dart, add a small one about midway between the neck and the armhole. It is also possible to correct this problem by simply adding a small shoulder pad to take up any extra fabric.

- SQUARE SHOULDERS (*usually indicated by wrinkles across the back below the neck*) SOLUTION: one correction is to cut the neckline deeper, which eliminates the wrinkles—but doesn't eliminate the problem! It is possible to adjust for square shoulders by working with your seam allowance. Starting with the normal allowance at the neckline, decrease your seam width gradually until you've gained a full ½″ (back and front) at the armhole (5). Try on the waist again. If it still pulls, it may be necessary to reduce the seam allowance for the sleeve section of the armhole, to give a little added width to the back.

[14]

- LARGE BOSOM *(indicated by diagonal wrinkle from bust to underarm side seam)* SOLUTION: often, changing the width and direction of the dart can correct bosom lines (6). For example, an angled dart beginning several inches above the waist may fit better than a horizontal dart at the bustline. If the bustline is low as well as large, it may be more flattering to eliminate any darts at the *waistline* and substitute gathers, or soft tucks, instead.

- SMALL BOSOM *(indicated by grain lines swinging down, instead of remaining even. The bodice will probably be too long at the center front waistline as well)* SOLUTION: shorten bodice front by making an even fold on the pattern grain about 2″ above the waistline. Decrease the underarm dart the same amount as the fold so that the side seams of the front and back bodice will match (7).

BOSOM

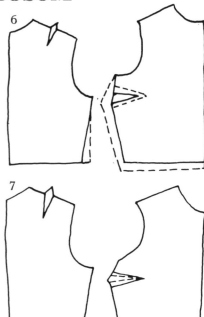

- LOW NECKLINE THAT GAPES SOLUTION: make an even vertical fold 2″ from the center line on each side. Adjust the slope of the neckline to accommodate the change (8). Try on again–the fold may have to be larger or smaller to eliminate the gape.

NECKLINE

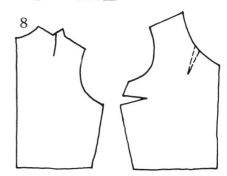

HOW TO FIT PANTS PROPERLY

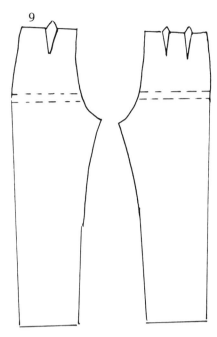

■ SOLUTION: to begin with, since waistlines are easier to adjust than the hipline, if possible buy your pants pattern according to the hip measurement. Check the pattern measurements very carefully and buy the size closest to your own hip dimensions.

   With pants or shorts, it's crucial to have a properly fitted muslin since many fitting points (crotch, derrière, thigh) cannot be changed after the face fabric is cut. After cutting your muslin from the pattern, here's how to make necessary adjustments:

■ CROTCH: If it has to be *shortened*, take a tuck in both front and back about 8″ down from the waist. You may be able to *lengthen* the crotch merely by utilizing some of your seam allowance at the waistline. If not, you'll have to add on extra fabric, both front and back, by slashing your muslin about 8″ down from the waist and joining on the necessary amount (9).

■ LEG LENGTH: Straight-legged pants can be lengthened or shortened by adding to or subtracting from the bottom hem. Flared-leg pants should be corrected about 8″ up from the hemline (10).

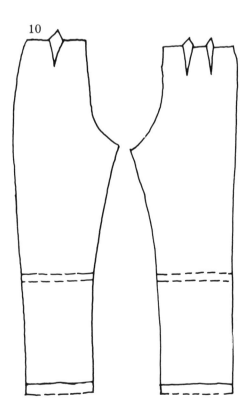

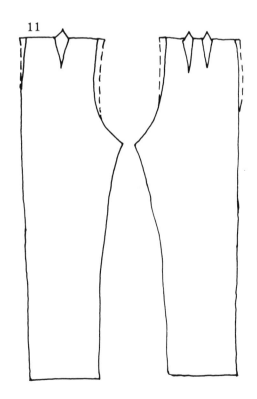

- WAISTLINES: These can be increased or decreased at side seams up to a total of 2″. To do this, divide the total amount you want to take in or let out by four. This amount is removed from or added to each side seamline, tapering to the hipline. (To take the maximum 2″ off, for example, you would remove ½″ from each side seam line.) If you need more than 2″, reduce the size of the waistline darts (11).

- THIGH WIDTH: To make pant legs fuller or slimmer, add to or subtract from the front and back pattern along the inside leg seam lines, beginning at the crotch and tapering to the lower edge (12, 13).

- DERRIÈRE: For a large derrière it may be enough simply to deepen and lengthen back darts, tapering to a point about 1″ above the fullest part of hips. Then compensate at waistline by adding necessary amount to the back side seams (14).

Couture Tip

- After establishing the proper alterations for your muslin, mark them with red chalk so you won't be confused by original markings. Then, as detailed in Chapter 4, take the muslin apart—either to use directly as a pattern, or as the basis for a paper pattern.

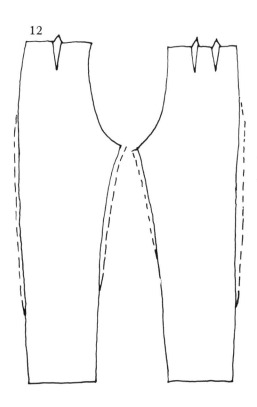

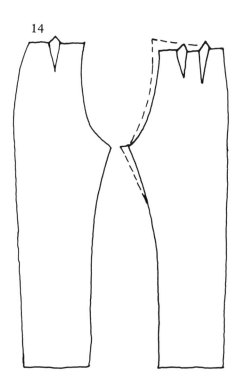

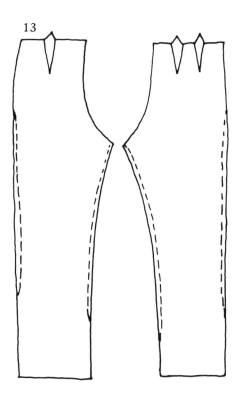

VI

Fabrics: The Catalyst to Fashion

THE plethora of fabulous fabrics available to home sewers today is enough to make your head swim. A walk through a well-stocked fabric department is almost intoxicating with wonderful textures, dazzling colors, artful prints, sophisticated go-togethers, all in a head-spinning harvest of natural fibers, synthetics and innumerable blends of both!

This splendid array is often so irresistible that many women are beginning to collect lovely fabrics the way wealthy people collect fine art! I caution against pell-mell fabric buying, however. First, you have to estimate the amount you may need, since you don't have a specific style in mind (and this can be costly, whether you over-buy or under-buy). Secondly, your tastes (and fashion's dictates) change and what looks wonderfully chic *this year* may seem déclassé next!

Although you should have the type of garment you want to make in mind (a dress, a coat, etc.), and a basic idea about the style, fabrics in themselves are tremendously inspiring and, often, spotting a certain fabric will change your idea about the design. (Professional designers always choose the fabric first and then let the fabric dictate the design.) Remember, the design you're burning to try may not be at all suitable for the fabric you're dying to buy! A very drapeable jersey, for example, is not meant for a straight-lined, close-fitting dress; a stiff linen won't work where soft fullness is needed.

SELECTING YOUR FABRICS

Here are a few facts to keep in mind when shopping:

1. Analyze your figure. If it's good—no problems.

Should it be found slightly wanting, you will naturally wish to conceal the worst part and emphasize the best.

2. Thick fabrics make you look larger; so will wild colors and large designs.

3. Don't let fabric overpower you. Even though your figure is perfect, if you're five feet tall, bold prints are out.

4. Clingy fabrics reveal every bulge, and care must be taken to work them in such a way that they'll drape softly, never fitting tightly, but just gliding over the body.

5. Fabrics that have body will tailor better than sleazy fabrics and present fewer problems. (Fabrics don't have to be heavy to have body—they must simply be firmly woven.) Certain chiffons have more body than others. You can tell only by feeling the fabric whether it has the necessary quality for your garment.

6. Often a fabric has to be built up with a firmer underlining to give it necessary body for your design. Most fabrics should be underlined. The weight of the underlining depends on the type of fabric and the design of the garment. A synthetic or rayon and cotton mixture is usually perfect for most fabrics, since it's available in soft, medium and heavy weight.

(Refer to chart for underlinings when making your selection.)

7. Always seek out quality. Bargain fabrics produce bargain-basement dresses. It takes just as much time and effort to work with shoddy material (often more time) as it does to work with the best —and the added expense of fine quality is more than made up for by the look and wearability of the end product.

8. Check all labels to see if the fabric has been pre-shrunk. Silks and some synthetic fabrics do not require shrinking; rayons, cottons, linens and wools need shrinking.

9. Determine the care factors—washable, permanent press, dry-clean only, etc.

A WORD ABOUT COLOR

Nothing is more exciting than color—and it's the first thing noticed about a new outfit. Certain colors provide a lift, make you feel important and even determine how you look. Color is definitely an inspiration when sewing and adds a great deal of enjoyment to any project.

Although not all colors are right for all people, it is easy to discover which colors suit you best—simply hold a length of fabric up to your face and judge. If it drains and subdues you, discard it. Does it lift and flatter you? It's yours! Keep trying though, and eliminate preconceived ideas about color. What is wrong now may be right three months from now. Keep in mind the function your proposed garment will play, too. A suit you plan to "live in" all season should be an easy-to-take color you won't tire of. On the other hand, a very special party dress that you'll wear only three or four times a year can be in a striking hue.

One very simple principle to remember vis-à-vis color: very bright colors will accentuate your size; duller and more subtle shades will minimize it.

PINPOINTING FABRIC TYPES

To tell you in detail the construction of various fabrics and the literally hundreds of different blend possibilities would require a separate textbook—a very technical textbook at that. For our purposes here, and your general knowledge, it's mainly important to know: Will the fabric be suitable for the item I want to make—will it tailor well?

Here is a brief guide to fabric types:

- WOOL: Easy to work with and shape; tailors well, must be pre-shrunk. Available in worsteds, tweeds, jerseys, knits, crepes and flannel.
  SILK: A luxury fabric used in expensive fashions; drapes well. Available in crepe, chiffon, jersey, organza, satin and some brocades.

- COTTON: Many different weights and weaves. Easy to work with, but 100 percent cotton has a tendency to wrinkle. Heavier-woven cottons will resist wrinkles better. There are many new cotton and synthetic-blend fabrics which give the look of cotton along with the high performance characteristics of man-made fibers.

[20]

- SYNTHETICS: The man-mades are miracle workers and very often several are used in the construction of a single fabric. Rayons and acetates resemble silk more closely than any other fabric, but when used alone have a tendency to wrinkle badly. (In combination with other fibers they are greatly wrinkle-resistant.) Polyesters, dacrons and nylons are easy to work with and care for; most are permanent press.

- KNITS: The most popular fabric type today! There are many, many different textures, weights and fibers—jacquards, wool, double knits, synthetic knits with the look and feel of matte jersey, lacy hand-knit-looks, stitching details, etc. Knits are fairly easy to work with, but are best stitched with a roller foot since this will not pull the threads or damage the material.

- FAKE FUR FABRICS: Effective-looking, fairly easy to work with. They must always be cut with nap running in one direction. Be careful about design chosen since furs look bulky.

- LACES: This feminine-looking fabric runs the gamut from modestly priced to true luxury. Lace is usually backed with tulle, chiffon or net; straight seams should be as fine and inconspicuous as possible. Often lace comes in a border which may be used at hemlines, necklines, etc.

- LEATHER-LIKE FABRICS: Usually vinyl or polyurethane coating over cotton, wool or synthetic. Although they require no special handling, a large stitch and "leather" needle are recommended. Keep your design simple, with as few seams as possible.

SUGGESTIONS FOR FABRIC USE

- COATS: tweeds, worsteds, heavy knits and wool jersey, firmly woven fabrics in wool or cotton; brocades, vinyls, fake furs.

- TAILORED DRESSES: worsted or firm wool crepe, wool jersey, woven cotton, linen, polyester fabrics, synthetic knits.

- SOFTER GARMENTS: crepe, matte jersey, soft polyester knits, thin wools or challis, lace, satin, chiffon.

- EVENING: crepe, organza, chiffon, chiffon brocades, matte jersey, velvet, brocades, lace.

■ Before you cut into your fabrics—outer fabric, underlining, interfacing—press each piece carefully with a pressing cloth and steam iron to be sure that it has been treated to maximum shrinkage. Also test to make sure the fabric doesn't have a special finish which will change the body of fabric when subjected to heat from ironing.

UNDERSTANDING THE GRAIN

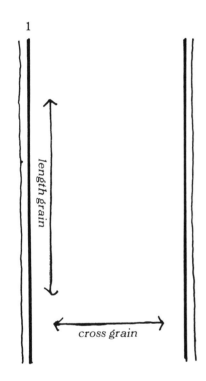

It's possible, of course, to casually cut into an expensive length of fabric without testing for perfect grain. But very "iffy." If the grain isn't exactly on target, you can wind up with a dress that rides up, pulls and twists and never hangs right. (And nothing in the world can correct the damage.) Since you're putting your all into the design and "manufacturing" of a couture dress, you must spend the appropriate amount of time on determining the grain.

All fabrics have three grains: lengthwise, cross and bias (1). The *lengthwise* grain runs along the selvage edge of the fabric and the border is a narrow pre-finished edge. *Cross* grain runs across the width of the fabric from selvage to selvage. *Bias* grain is cut on a 45-degree angle from any two straight edges.

FINDING THE LENGTH-WISE GRAIN

Most apparel is cut on the lengthwise grain, since the fabric drapes better and has a better hang. To establish true lengthwise grain, fasten fabric to cutting board with tailor's push pins, fastening selvage edges together, right side in. Also pin any torn or cut edges together. (The selvage and/or torn edge should be parallel to the edge of cutting board to be sure grain is right.)

Sometimes a fabric can be stretched back on grain by pulling across the bias.

Next pull or press the fabric into shape so that it's "on grain" without puckers or wrinkles, pulling on the bias grain to straighten. Steam press fabric while on the board, but don't press the center fold, since resulting crease is difficult to remove.

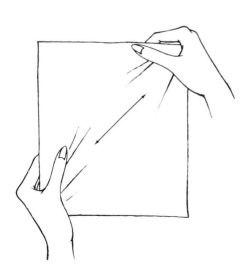

FINDING THE CROSS GRAIN

One easy way of determining cross grain is to pick up one of the strands of fiber from the selvage and gently pull it out of the fabric, working your way from one end of the selvage to the other (2). This will indicate perfectly even weave. (However, this cannot be done with knits or with some very tightly woven fabrics.) With some fabrics it is also possible to tear carefully from selvage to selvage in order to straighten the fabric end.

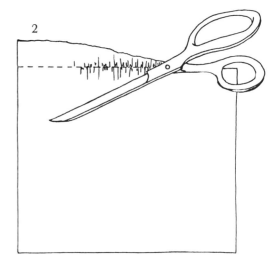

FINDING THE BIAS GRAIN

Bias grain has the most elasticity and is always used for pipings and bindings. This grain is a diagonal intersection between the lengthwise and crosswise threads of the material (3). It molds to any shape and is generally used to cut interfacings. Although some dresses are cut on the bias they are difficult to work and require a very experienced sewer. (They do hang beautifully and softly and mold well to the figure, however.) To achieve perfect bias, use a triangular ruler and place it on the straight lengthwise and crosswise grain.

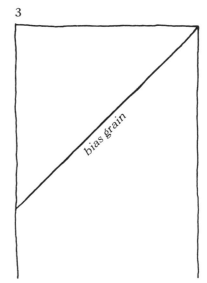

Couture Tips

▪ If synthetic fabrics run off grain they cannot be pulled back on grain. Perfect grain is not absolutely necessary for this type of fabric. You can cut the material by matching the selvage edge of the fabric and trimming evenly the cut or cross-grain edge.

▪ Some fabrics have a tendency to pull up at the selvage. This can be overcome by clipping the selvage edge every 8″ or 10″ to help it lie flat.

The Shape of Fashion: Underlinings, Interfacings

VII

IF you really want to design and make couturier clothes, you have to carry through from the inside out—face value efforts are not for you! Forget the idea of a sew-and-go dress. Instant fashion—like instant coffee—is a substitute, but that's all. It can't be the real thing.

For the real thing in fashion, it's necessary to take all the proper steps to make the final product truly notable. It's the concentration on preparation that counts. To include another analogy: in creating a gourmet dinner, so much more time goes into planning, preparing and shepherding the meal from start to serving than actually enters into the enjoyment of that meal. So it is with couture sewing.

We're talking about the behind-the-scenes work of such vital helpers as underlinings, facings and interfacings.

UNDERSTANDING UNDERLININGS

Underlinings give better hang to a garment, more body and conceal the stitching of facings and hems. Underlining also reduces wrinkles in clothes and results in overall improved wearability. There are many excellent easy-to-work-with materials available today, most of them man-made synthetics combined with cotton and other natural fibers. They usually come in three weights to accommodate most fabric types—lightweight, medium and heavy.

An old favorite, China silk, is good with certain

soft fabrics, but it has a tendency to shift and is a little more difficult to work with. Organza handles well, but unfortunately doesn't wear well. Remember that your underlining should never be heavier than the face fabric, unless you are trying to build greater body. If your fabric is supple, the underlining should be supple so it doesn't interfere with the drapeability of the face fabric.

Shaping and inner construction of a garment make the difference between couture and boutique clothes: therefore, great attention must be paid to the suitability of the lining chosen. (A complete guide is given at the end of this chapter.) Remember, the underlining also acts as your pattern. As noted in Chapter 8, the pattern is placed directly on the underlining and all construction markings transferred to the underlining.

Couture Tips on Underlinings

■ Heavy wools require underlining to conceal the stitching, not to provide extra body; a lightweight choice is adequate.

■ Permanent press pleated skirts should *not* be underlined.

■ Stretch fabrics should *not* be underlined.

■ Double knits should *not* be underlined.

■ Crepe or thin wool pleated skirts should be underlined before the skirt is pleated. (Butterfly or China silk is excellent for this use.)

■ Sheer fabrics (organza or lace) should be underlined in organza to give the garment a better finished look.

■ Chiffon cannot be underlined in anything but chiffon and that only for the bodice. Chiffon skirts should have more than one layer–the more the better–each one separate from the other.

■ Wool jersey or matte jersey may be tailored by lining with China silk for the bodice. Do not line the sleeves. Sew the skirt lining separately and attach only at the waistline. If, however, you want a soft look with jerseys, *don't* line them.

■ Washable polyester fabrics should *not* be underlined.

■ Washable knit fabrics should *not* be underlined.

FACTS ABOUT FACINGS

Facings are the inside sections of a garment that must be made in the face fabric since they are sometimes obvious—i.e., the "wrong" side of a jacket closing, the inside of a collar, etc.

Front facings may be cut in three different ways:

1. If the garment has a straight front closing, the facing can be extended to be included and cut in one piece with the front section. This facing will take the shape of the garment and extend into the neckline and shoulder seam (1).

2. If you have a curved lapel on the garment, the facing can be cut in one with the garment from the hem to the point where the lapel *starts* (2). This all-in-one section is then joined at this point to an extra facing that will take the shape of the lapel and extend into the neckline and part of the shoulder. This additional part of the facing will be stitched to the lapel, right sides together, to form a seam on the edge of the lapel (3).

3. The facing can be cut as a completely separate unit (4) and attached to the front of the garment from hem to neck with a seam on the edge (5).

Couture Tips on Front Facings

■ If not extended on the original pattern, separate facings are usually included in the pattern envelope. (If not, cut one in the same shape as the section to be faced.) Always stitch the joining seams of the facing and press open before attaching to garment.

■ To attach, place facings right sides together on garment, pin and baste, then stitch. Trim seams, turn facing to wrong side, pulling out edges and favoring the right side by a hairline so that the seam will not be obvious from the right side. Understitching, by hand, close to seam on the seam allowance will keep the facing from "rolling out." Baste the edge and steam lightly.

■ The cut edge of a facing can be finished with bias seam binding or bias lace edging and attached to underlining. (For an unlined garment, use bias seam binding.) If fabric is thin, you may turn under a small hem and machine stitch close to the edge of the fold line. Slip-stitch this "hem" to underlining.

[26]

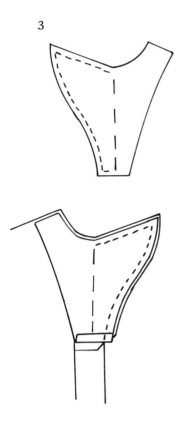

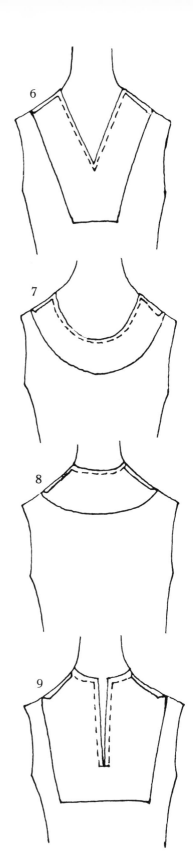

Couture Tips on Neckline Facings

- Your pattern will include the unit for the neckline facing. If it doesn't, make the facing from the same pattern used to cut the waist, utilizing only the neck and shoulder section (6–9).

- Stitch the shoulder seams and press open. With right sides together attach to the neckline of garment: pin, matching center front, shoulder seams and notches. Baste, then stitch.

- Clip center front and curved areas. Turn to the wrong side. Baste around neckline, pulling seam under a hairline so seam will not show on the edge. Understitch if necessary. Finish cut edge with bias seam binding and blind stitch to underlining. Press lightly.

- If fabric is too heavy to make a self-facing, use a taffeta in the same color as face fabric, matching as closely as possible.

- If wool is scratchy use taffeta.

- If fabric has no body, it's advisable to put an extra layer of Siri or heavy Si Bonne on the facing before attaching to garment.

- The same technique is applied to all necklines and all shapes such as V-shaped, oval, round, square, slashed or high.

- For low necks it's a good idea to stitch a seam binding on the stitching line to keep it from stretching.

IMPORTANCE OF INTERFACINGS

Interfacings are usually cut in the shape of a facing and placed between facing and garment (or underlining). In addition to adding strength to such stress areas as closings, pockets and flaps, they shape collars, give weight to cuffs, prevent waistbands from stretching. Interfacings are generally

[28]

made of tailor's canvas, Hymo or Siri; the weight selected is determined by the weight of the outer fabric and the areas where it is used. It is also determined by the amount of firmness required.

Couture Tips on Interfacings

■ For coats and suits a woven tailor's hair canvas is best, since it lends itself to tailoring and will mold to the shape of the garment (10). This interfacing, usually cut on the bias grain, will take the curve of a seam when applied to the outer fabric. Some coats require an extra bias fold of canvas in the fold line of the hem to keep it from "breaking."

■ In coat dresses or shirtwaist dresses, a medium or firm Siri can be substituted to keep the collar and cuffs from collapsing and give the facings a well-tailored, rounded look (11, 12). Siri can also be used in the fold line of the hem.

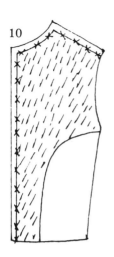

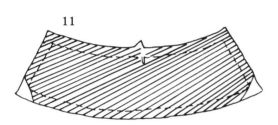

GUIDE FOR LININGS, INTERFACINGS

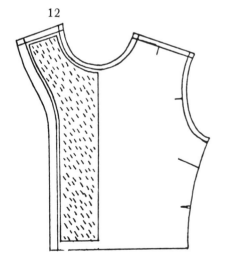

FABRIC	UNDERLINING	INTERFACING
heavy woolens	light Si Bonne Undercurrent lightweight synthetic	heavy or medium tailor's canvas or Hymo
medium-weight woolens	lightweight Undercurrent or Si Bonne; China silk, Butterfly or other synthetic	medium canvas or heavy Siri
lightweight woolens	medium Si Bonne or Undercurrent; China silk, Butterfly synthetic	medium canvas or Siri
heavy cotton or synthetics	lightweight Si Bonne or Undercurrent synthetic	heavy Siri
medium cotton silk, synthetics	lightweight Si Bonne; organza, Undercurrent synthetic	lightweight Siri
knits, jersey	China silk or Butterfly	
washable	washable synthetic	

VIII Cutting: A Labor of Love

SINCE a slip of the scissors can mean disaster, it's important to substitute skill for luck when you are ready to attack fabric with shears. Again, time and patience are crucial. Don't just plunge in—it's necessary to study your pattern pieces carefully, and make sure your layout is absolutely accurate before snipping off even one little facing.

PRELIMINARY STEPS

1. If you are using a fitted muslin as your pattern, make sure all your alteration markings are clearly indicated and that the muslin is pressed.

2. If you are using a paper pattern, the print side should face up. Don't reverse any units in a pattern to save fabric or to accommodate a particular layout. You might wind up with a garment you cannot put together!

3. As previously indicated, before cutting, press the face fabrics as well as underlining and tailor's canvas to insure that all fabrics have been subjected to maximum shrinkage.

CUTTING THE UNDERLINING

Since most garments are underlined, the proper approach to cutting is to place the pattern directly on the underlining.

1. Fold the underlining in half and pin selvage edges together. Be sure the lining is on grain. If center front of the garment has no seam, place pattern with center front on fold of material. Lay out entire pattern before cutting, and secure to cutting board with push pins. Each piece of the pattern

should be secured to cutting board. This will keep the fabric and pattern from shifting.

2. To be sure you are on straight grain, measure each end of grain line indicated on your pattern from selvage edge of fabric. Repeat this for all parts of pattern where grain line is indicated.

3. If you are working with a bias grain, use a triangular ruler, placed on the straight grain of fabric to give you perfect bias (1).

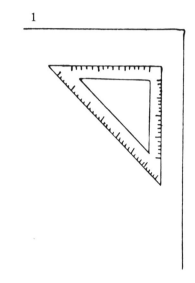

4. If the fabric is not sufficient to cut all pieces on the double, cut as many pieces as you can on the double first; then open the material and cut the remaining pieces. (Each pattern will indicate how many times a unit, such as pockets or trim, has to be cut.)

5. All construction lines and symbols must be transferred to underlining. You can do this by inserting a piece of dressmaker's tracing paper between the underlining fabric and the paper pattern, carbon side toward fabric. Note: when using dressmaker's tracing paper or tracing chalk, try to get a color close to the fabric shade. Always test the tracing paper and chalk on a scrap of fabric to see if it stains when pressed.

6. Patterns all have construction markings and symbols which serve an important purpose in every phase of constructing and sewing your garment. With these construction symbols you are guided toward giving your garment proper form and shape. Every symbol means something, from seam lines to center fold lines, grain lines, collar mounting lines, buttonholes and pocket placement lines. Therefore, when transferring your pattern markings to underlining, be sure not to eliminate any.

7. Go over all construction lines, darts, center line, buttonhole lines, collar mounting lines, cross marks, etc., to be sure underlining is clearly marked. (Couture clothes are worked with cross marks instead of notches. Cross marks are an extension of the notches, extending about 2″ via a running stitch on the right side of fabric [2].) Use a transparent ruler or tracing wheel for this. Incidentally, if your dress or garment is unlined,

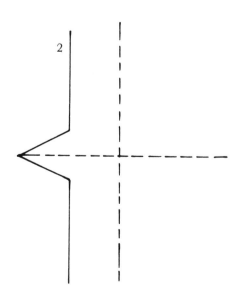

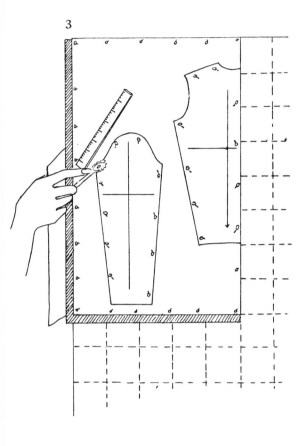

simply follow the same procedure as described here, transferring all construction lines directly to the wrong side of outer fabric.

8. When you have completely traced the pattern on one side of the underlining, remove pattern carefully, replacing pins on the fabric so that you can trace the underlayer of the lining (3). Place the tracing paper under the bottom layer, carbon side toward fabric, and retrace with tracing wheel all the markings on the lining, shifting the carbon tracing paper until all construction lines and symbols are transferred to the underlayer of the fabric. Now you can cut the underlining.

Couture Tips before Cutting the Face Fabric

■ For synthetic fabrics, ascertain whether the crease in the fold line can be removed by pressing —very often the crease in man-made fabrics is permanent. If the pattern calls for pieces to be placed on the fold line, and the fabric is not wide enough to shift the fold line so that it will not interfere with the pattern, then cut the fabric open—or choose a pattern which will be adaptable to your fabric.

■ Some fabrics have a right and wrong side; others can be used on either side, but when you are cutting a design, it should all be cut on the *same* side to avoid shading.

■ When cutting knits or jerseys, don't stretch the fabric. It should lie flat without tension on your cutting board.

■ Fabrics with nap must be cut with all pattern pieces placed in *one direction,* usually with the nap running down for a smoother touch and to keep fabric from "roughing up." Velvets are generally cut to give the darkest, richest shading—this could mean either up or down.

■ Some smooth surface wools also shade when held in opposite directions. Insure uniformity by holding the fabric up in both directions together to determine if it shades. If so, the fabric must be cut in one direction; if not, it's safe to cut either up or down.

■ Fabrics with a definite design may have to be cut

on the right side in order to match the design. Study your pattern well after you lay it out and check seam joinings to see if they will match correctly when stitched (4). This requires great concentration–don't try to hurry through the procedure. (You can simplify the matching problem by selecting a pattern with as few seams as possible.) Always allow sufficient extra yardage, since there will be some waste when matching design.

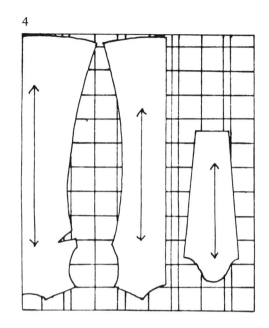

■ Very often the most expensive fabrics are printed off grain. This can be true in plaids or prints with a definite straight design. If this is the case, you are better off rejecting this fabric as it is virtually impossible to match–and your resulting dress will always look crooked.

■ In cutting prints it is sometimes necessary to shift a pattern an entire repeat in order to match. This could involve as much as 30″, depending on the repeat interval.

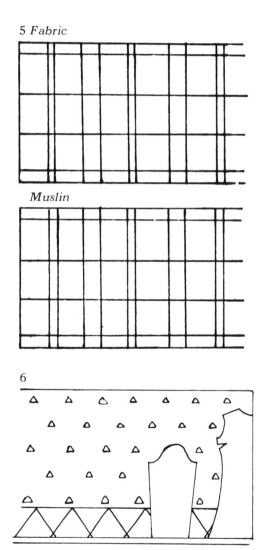

5 *Fabric*

Muslin

■ To cut plaids without making an error, an excellent approach is to mark your muslin fabric (before cutting) with the same principal plaid lines as the face fabric, making sure the lines on the muslin correspond to the lines of the plaid (5). Cut the muslin and put it together to determine whether all seams match, including sleeves. If they do, it is safe to place the muslin directly on the face fabric, matching design pattern, and cut from this muslin.

■ Stripes can be both even and uneven, similar to plaids. Follow procedure outlined for plaids, above. Avoid placing darts on most noticeable stripe. Make sure stripes are directly over one another on both layers of fabric and pin layers together along stripe line to prevent shifting during cutting. Uneven stripes should be cut with pattern pieces pointed in one direction, as for napped fabrics.

■ Usually border prints must be cut on the cross grain since the border is always placed along the selvage edge and runs the length of the fabric. Your pattern must then be matched from the edge of the border up because this is the focal point of the design (6). Be sure to ascertain the correct length of your garment before laying out your pattern, since

the hemline has already been decreed by the border and you cannot easily lengthen or shorten without distorting the border. (If you need to shorten, before cutting take a fold just above the border of your pattern to the correct length; to lengthen, cut through the pattern just above the border and allow the necessary inches.)

CUTTING THE FACE FABRIC

1. Always fold your fabric right side *in* when cutting, except for definite designs, plaids or stripes, as described above.

2. Pin your underlining to the wrong side of the outer fabric, using the underlining as a pattern. Measure all grain lines as you did for the underlining and place the entire lining on the outer fabric before you start to cut. Be sure your fabrics are well fastened to cutting board so they will not shift.

3. Cut the outer fabric, then separate the lining from the outer fabric so that you will be working with a single layer of material.

4. Pin each unit of the underlining to the *wrong* side of the outer fabric, matching each unit; be sure lining is taut and does not wrinkle or pucker.

5. Run a small basting stitch over all construction lines, cross marks, etc., including center grain lines, buttonholes, collar mounting lines, through to the outer layer of fabric so that all markings will clearly show on the *right* side of the outer fabric.

6. Center line should be basted and remain so until garment is finished.

All about Stitches and Seams

IX

BEFORE you begin the actual construction of your couture garment, you will have to take a quick course in the various types of hand stitches, as well as the machine-type seaming required to turn your new design into a custom-made dream. Learn the distinctions among each of the following—and use each technique well:

BASTING STITCH: a temporary stitch to hold two pieces of fabric together. Used to indicate construction markings when transferring pattern to fabric. A basting stitch can be small or large depending on how it is used. To indicate construction markings, it should be no longer than ¾″ (1).

SLIP BASTING: used for joining two pieces of fabric together on the right side. Turn under one seam allowance and lap it over the seam allowance on the opposite side, matching seam markings and cross marks. Pin at intervals with pins placed diagonally to the seam. Slip needle through from edge of top fold to fabric underneath, making sure thread goes through underlining to form a straight basting stitch about ⅜″ long (2).

SLIP STITCH: used for finishing facings, hems, patch pockets, coats and suit linings, banded trims, etc. Slide the needle through edge of fold and pick up a thread or two of the under fabric. Keep stitches about ¼″ apart (3).

HAND-TAILORING TECHNIQUES

1 BASTING STITCH

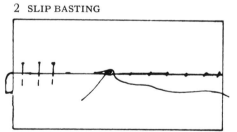

2 SLIP BASTING

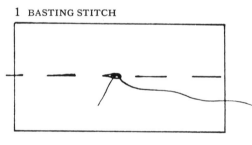

3 SLIP STITCH

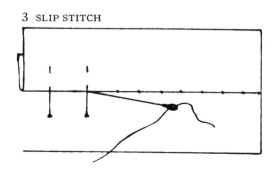

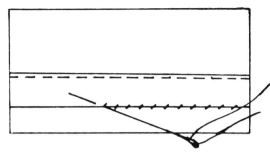

4 HEMMING STITCH

HEMMING STITCH: used to finish zipper tapes, facings and hems when edged with a seam binding. Can be used in place of slip stitch on any thin fabric. Make close stitches, catching a thread of the under fabric and sliding the needle under the seam binding about 1/16″ from the top. This will form a slanted stitch on the seam binding (4).

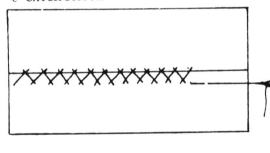

5 BLIND STITCH

BLIND STITCH: used for hems. It is placed about ¼″ below finished edge. Catch upper, then lower fabric with the needle, forming a slanted stitch similar to a catch stitch (5).

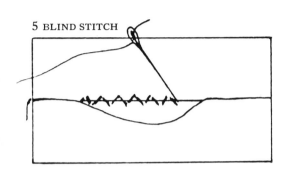

6 CATCH STITCH

CATCH STITCH: used for attaching edge of interfacing to fabric on collars, facings, pockets, etc. Start sewing from left to right; take a short stitch on interfacing ¼″ down from edge, then a short stitch on fabric, catching one or two threads. Keep stitches about ¼″ apart and slanted (6).

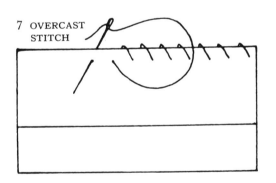

7 OVERCAST STITCH

OVERCAST STITCH: used for finishing seam edges. It keeps the fabric from raveling and makes a neat finish. Run a machine stitch about ⅛″ down from edge of seam allowance. Slide the needle under the machine stitch and over the edge of the material to make a slanted stitch (7).

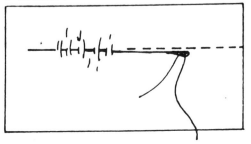

8 RUNNING STITCH

RUNNING STITCH: a small straight stitch used to indicate cross marks on the right side of the fabric as an extension of the construction notches. Also employed for hand shirring and easing. Take several stitches on the needle before pulling thread through the stitches. A running stitch is the most commonly used stitch for all kinds of hand sewing. It can be combined with a back stitch for extra strength (8).

[36]

SHIRRING STITCH: a loose double hand or machine stitch leaving thread ends on each side so that fullness can be adjusted to fit area. Threads should be tied after shirring is adjusted (9).

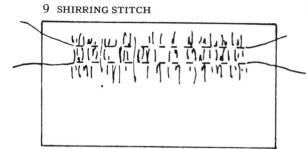

9 SHIRRING STITCH

PADDING STITCH: used to attach interfacings to collars, cuffs, pockets and facings. It is a diagonal stitch, caught to underlining of unit. The length of the stitch depends on where it is used. It's closer and shorter, about ½″ long, on the roll lines of lapels and collars; lighter and longer on other areas, about 1″ long (10).

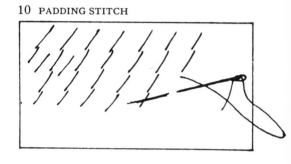

10 PADDING STITCH

ZIGZAG STITCH: alternate stitch to padding. Can be used for same purpose (11).

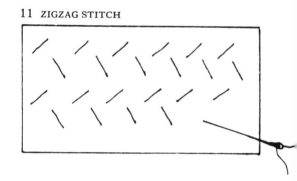

11 ZIGZAG STITCH

HAND PICKING: used for hand-sewing zippers. Also used for detail on any finished edge such as pockets, collars, etc. It is a back stitch that picks up just two or three threads, but must go through the under fabric. Each stitch is placed ⅛″ or ¼″ apart (12).

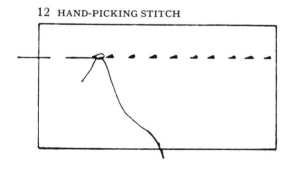

12 HAND-PICKING STITCH

[37]

MACHINE-STITCH-ING TIPS

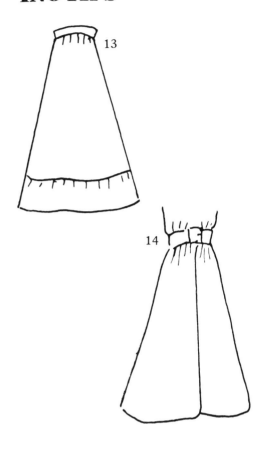

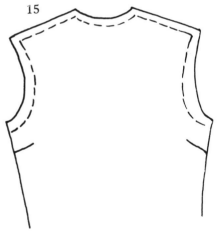

EASE STITCHING: used to control the fullness on the cut edge of an A-line hem; also for the double row of stitches on the cap of the sleeve. These should be ¼″ apart and 3″ or 4″ of the thread should be allowed after sewing to pull the stitches for proper adjusting to armhole (13).

SHIRRING: to gather a waistline of a skirt, loosen the upper tension so that the bobbin thread will pull easily to adjust for the fullness required. Always run a double shirring stitch ¼″ apart. Pull both bobbin threads at the same time. After you have determined the amount of fullness necessary, tie the thread ends to secure them (14).

STAY STITCHING: a single line of stitching placed about ½″ from the edge in areas that are not on straight grain, such as necklines, armholes, shoulders or curved edges. This will keep the fabric from stretching while you are working on the garment. It is the first step in construction. Be sure not to pull the fabric while stay stitching (15).

16 ZIGZAG STITCHES

ZIGZAG STITCHES: zigzagging stitches are used to finish seam edges to prevent raveling. However, couturiers never use this finish—instead, they either overcast by hand or run a double machine stitch on the edge. There is nothing wrong with using a zigzag finish on seams, especially for knits. Couturiers use the other method chiefly because of habit and also most of the professional machines are older and do not have the same innovations (16).

HOW TO FINISH A SEAM

OVERCASTING: method used by French and American couturiers (17).

17 OVERCASTING

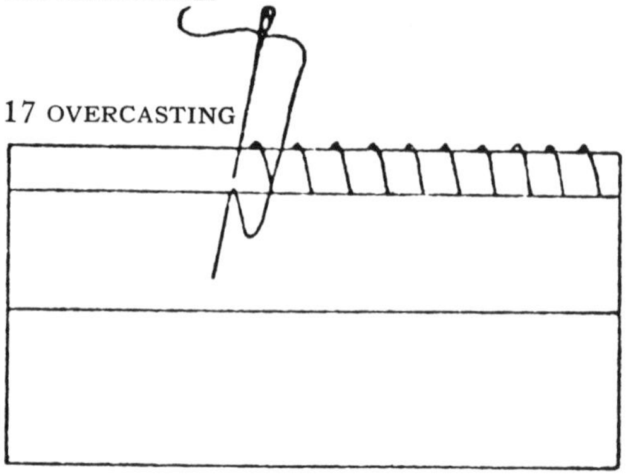

DOUBLE STITCHING: run a double machine stitch about ¼″ from cut edge of seam allowance (18).

18 DOUBLE STITCHING

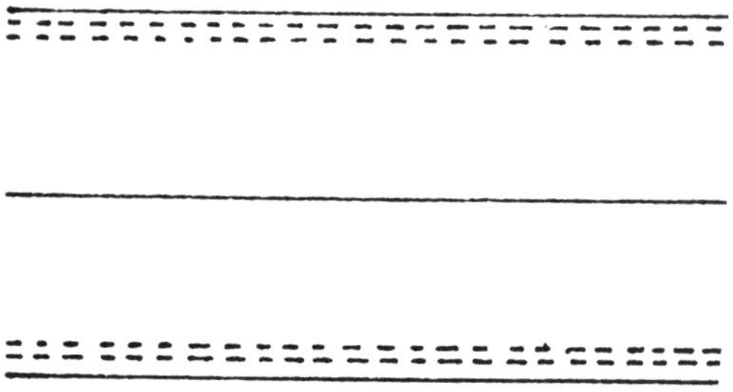

19 TURNED-UNDER HEM

TURNED-UNDER HEM: if fabric is lightweight, turn under a very small hem and machine stitch close to the edge of the fold (19, 20).

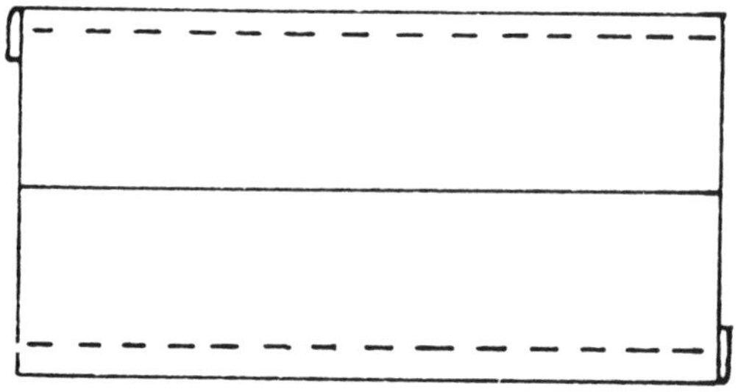

20

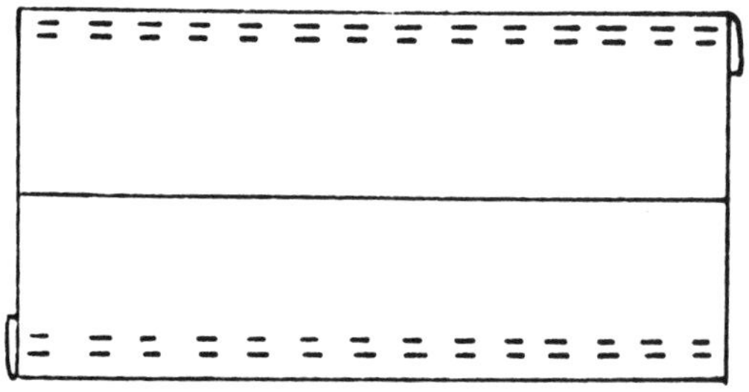

BOUND SEAMS: place a bias seam binding over edge of seam allowance, the same width on each side. Run a machine stitch near edge of seam binding, catching both edges with the same row of stitches (21).

21 BOUND SEAMS

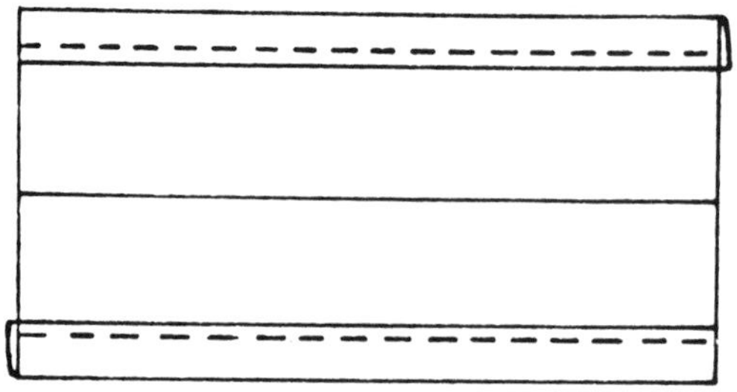

[39]

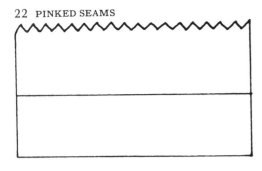

22 PINKED SEAMS

PINKED SEAMS: where there is an extra lining in the garment and the seams are concealed, the seam allowance can be pinked with a pinking shears (22).

FRENCH SEAMS: used for very sheer fabrics and curtains. Stitch a narrow seam, *wrong* sides together. Trim to ⅛"; press to one side. Turn right sides together, press fold and stitch again, ¼" from fold lines (23).

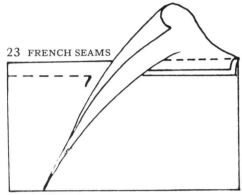

23 FRENCH SEAMS

There are other methods of finishing a seam, but these are the ones most commonly used by the couturier and all you will ever really need.

Couture Tips

▪ Clipped or notched seams are a must for collars, necklines, waistlines or any curved seams, to give them a spread and keep the garment from puckering (24).

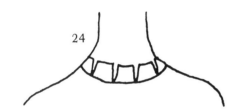

24

▪ A notch is a straight cut, not a wedge cut. If necessary, a seam can be notched to within ⅛" from the stitching line.

SEAMS USED AS DETAIL

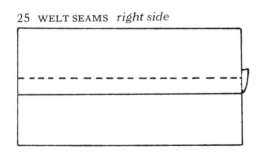

25 WELT SEAMS *right side*

WELT SEAM: After stitching seam, press to one side. On right side of garment, run a machine stitch parallel to the seam through both seam allowances. The distance from the seam is determined by the width of the welt desired (25).

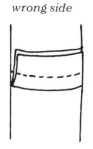

wrong side

DOUBLE WELT SEAM: stitch and press seam open. On right side of fabric, run a machine stitch the same distance from the seam on both sides. If you want the welt to be raised, insert a strip of bias cotton flannel under the seam allowance; baste in place before stitching on the right side of fabric (26).

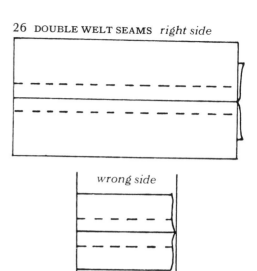

26 DOUBLE WELT SEAMS *right side*

wrong side

SLOT SEAM: Stitch seam with large stitches (to be removed later) and press open. Place a strip of self fabric on wrong side the same length as the seam and a little wider than the two seam allowances and baste on both edges. On right side, run a machine stitch equal distance from the seam on both sides. Remove the stitches from the temporary seam (27).

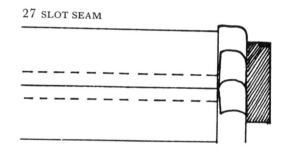

27 SLOT SEAM

TOP STITCH: Top stitch is used on any finished edge, such as collars, facings, pockets or any other seamed area to be outlined as detail (28, 29).

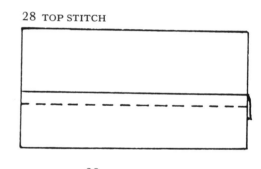

28 TOP STITCH

29

PIPING: Bias grain is always used for this edging or trimming on a garment. It can be self or contrasting color or material. True bias must be used to keep the binding from twisting. Piping can also be inserted between the garment and the facing. It can be flat or corded (30).

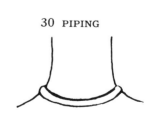

30 PIPING

[41]

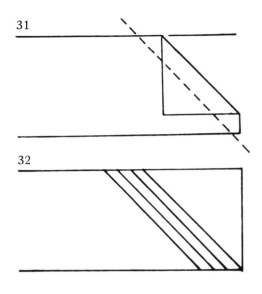

31

32

If the fabric is wide enough to permit the piping to be made in one piece, so much the better (31); if not the strips will have to be joined on the bias grain before sewing to the garment (32). Piping or binding is stitched right sides together, then turned and finished on the wrong side with a hemming stitch. Measure the piping so it will be even in width before sewing.

Measure the width of each strip by marking both ends and connecting with a yardstick and chalk. Allow ¼″ on each side of the strip for seaming. Cut the strips on the chalk mark and seam together on the bias grain. Do not match the outer edge; just the seam allowance.

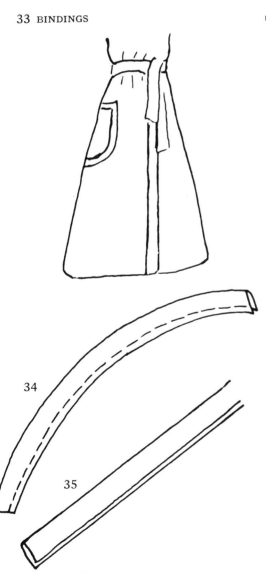

33 BINDINGS

34

35

• BINDINGS: Bindings can be a very decorative addition to a garment (33). If you are using a wide binding, you can usually shape the binding to the curve of the area in which you're using it. Fold the bias strip in half, form a curve on the ironing board, steam lightly and pat down with the palm of your hand. Bias has elasticity, and you can easily shape the fabric in this way (34).

To form a sharp corner with binding, unless you are using a knit or jersey fabric, the binding must be mitered on the top side and again on the underside. The principle of mitering a corner binding is the same as mitering a seam (see below), but with binding, the process has to be done twice. Since this is difficult and requires very precise workmanship, if possible, round to corners on binding to avoid the miter.

If the fabric you're using is thin, make binding of double material. Cut a bias strip twice the desired width, fold in half and press on fold line (35). Pin the cut edge of fold to cut edge of garment on right side; pin and baste, then stitch. Turn to wrong side and finish with a hemming stitch on folded edge.

Don't trim the garment any shorter than the fold line of the binding. The material left in the middle of the binding is what gives you a nice rounded or heavier-looking binding.

MITERING A SEAM: Mitering a seam involves joining two seam allowances to form a neat square corner. Turn both seam allowances up and press. Open out the fold and with a ruler mark a diagonal line running through the point where the two creases meet. Trim excess fabric ¼" from mark (36).

Fold the corners (37); with right sides together baste and stitch on the ¼" marking line (38). Trim corners to the point. Next, press seam open. Turn to right side and press (39).

■ MITERING A BAND: To miter a band before stitching to garment, form a right angle by crossing both bands. Draw a diagonal line through the point where both bands cross. Trace line with tracing paper to underlayer of band. Allow ¼" seam on each band and cut. Pin and baste on the wrong side; stitch and press open (40).

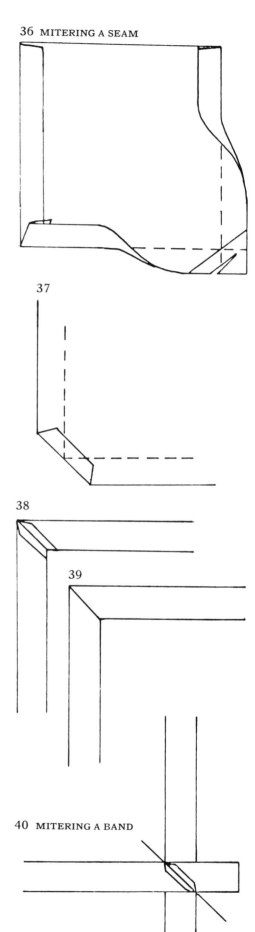

36 MITERING A SEAM

37

38

39

40 MITERING A BAND

[43]

Ironclad Rule: Press as You Sew

x

AS you know by now, this is not a book about shortcuts—this is a manual for *couture* sewing. And an ironclad, absolutely unbreakable rule you must observe is: *press* every step of the way! Following is the equipment you need—and the how-to for professional pressing:

EQUIPMENT

A GOOD STEAM IRON: the invention of the steam iron was a boon, not only to the family laundress (*you!*), but also to the do-it-yourself couturière. Make sure your iron works properly and is clean— if it sticks at all, iron it over some waxed paper to renew the slickness.

IRONING BOARD: with a good padded cover. Throw out that old burned one and buy a perky, gay new one. Ironing (for any project) will seem like less of a bore, and you will have better results with a smooth cover.

SLEEVE BOARD: indispensable for short seams, sleeves and details that are awkward to handle on the "big board."

TAILOR'S HAM: molds and shapes curved areas, especially important when working on suits and coats.

POUNDING BLOCK: another must for expert tailoring; ideal for opening seams and flattening edges.

PRESS CLOTH: prevents shine on the right side of fabric, usually made of heavy pressing cotton. (Can also be lighter-weight cotton material over wool.) A press cloth will not mat down woolen or spongy fabrics and is excellent for pressing coats or suits.

[44]

SEAMS: should be pressed with the grain. (For fabrics that might mark on the right side, slip a piece of cardboard between the seam allowance and garment before ironing.) Seams are usually pressed open; curved seams should be ironed over a tailor's ham to keep the sewn-in shape. If extra moisture is needed, use your steam or a damp pressing cloth over a dry one. Make sure the fabric doesn't spot when exposed to water—and be sure the iron isn't so hot that the fabric will dry immediately. Top-stitched or welted seams are always pressed flat; French seams are pressed flat with the wider seam edge ironed over the trimmed seam edge before the second stitching.

DARTS: should be pressed over a tailor's ham to minimize the point. Bust, shoulder and waistline darts are usually pressed toward the center of the garment; and elbow darts are usually pressed *down*.

SHIRRING OR RUFFLES: should never be pressed flat. Lift fabric while you're pressing; use the tip of the iron for that soft touch.

SLEEVES: armhole seams are pressed toward the sleeves, using the edge of the iron, gently. To shrink out ease at the shoulder line, use a tailor's ham.

Couture Tips About Special Fabrics

▪ Your steam iron will usually offer a capsule guide about proper temperatures for fabric types. Obey it well—you can ruin all your efforts if you press at the wrong heat level.

▪ Cottons, linens will usually respond well to "steam heat." If not, use a damp pressing cloth or dampened wash cloth.

▪ Corduroys, velvets—use a medium warm iron; avoid crushing the pile or nap. A velvet press board should be used for velvet.

▪ Knits, jerseys—use a medium-hot iron on the wrong side of the fabric. Press on the lengthwise grain; be careful about stretching the fabric. Many knits and jerseys made with synthetic fibers need very little ironing.

▪ Silks should be ironed very lightly over press cloth with a medium-hot temperature and a very little amount of steam.

■ Woolens should be pressed with a wool press cloth, or thin cotton over wool, *always* with a steam iron. Very often steam from the iron is sufficient for smoothing edges, which should not be pressed too flat—merely pound edges down with a pounding block or the palm of your hand. The iron should not touch the fabric as this pressing is usually done on the right side and "direct contact" would leave marks.

■ Always pre-test all fabrics before actual sewing to make sure that maximum shrinkage has been achieved, and to determine the proper temperature for subsequent bouts with the iron.

■ Never press over pins. If you press over basting stitches, do so lightly; then remove stitches and press area again to eliminate the stitch marks.

■ For thin fabrics, a cheesecloth folded three or four times will do the same work as a press cloth.

■ To finish shirring or ruffles only the *stitched* area should be pressed flat, to avoid bulk when sewing to another unit of garment.

■ Buttonholes should be pressed with a cardboard under the strips to prevent the press marks from showing through on the right side of fabric. This technique also applies to ironing zippers. If pressing on the right side is required, use the same cardboard under the seams, *but* always use a press cloth as well.

■ When pressing a hem, never iron the edge directly. Simply steam and pat down with the palm of your hand. Don't put your iron on the cut edge after it is sewn to the dress—this will surely leave a mark on the right side of the fabric. As mentioned in the section on hems, if there is extra fullness on the cut edge of hem, this should be steamed and fullness shrunken-in before sewing on seam binding and hemming.

■ If you are pressing any areas where the fabric is double-thickness, such as flap pockets, use a cardboard under the pocket, and a press cloth on top of the right side of fabric.

■ Always allow fabric to dry before removing it from pressing board.

Couture Constructions: Know-How in Depth

XI

YOU may be thinking—*now* we're ready to sew. But are you? Your pattern has been faithfully and accurately transposed to fabric; appropriate underlinings, facings and interfacings are marked and ready-to-sew; equipment is at hand and in working order. As I've said from the start, however, in couture sewing there is only one way to go: the right way. Don't sew one stitch until you've assimilated the couturier techniques for all the different components that make or break the way your garment will look: darts, sleeves, necklines, collars, pockets, buttonholes, zippers, hems, ruffles and belts.

Consider the time spent learning how to execute each of these details accurately and professionally as money in the bank toward your own personal best-dressed wardrobe.

Darts are easier said than done. A seemingly simple technique, they mean so much in overall fitting and creating contour. Follow this procedure to score a bull's-eye:

1. Darts should always be stitched starting at the wide end and finishing at the point. Thread should be tied at both ends. It is best to press a dart using a tailor's ham so that you can retain the shape, eliminate the point and avoid wrinkling the surrounding fabric.

2. Many patterns have very long darts extending over the bust. In my opinion, these detract from the beauty of a garment. Darts can easily be shortened without spoiling the fit. Simply place the ruler 1″ to

DARTS DO IT

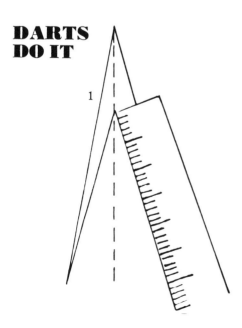

1½″ back from the center line of dart to outside marking at the seam and draw a new line. Repeat on opposite side (1).

3. Sometimes it's better to curve a dart slightly, especially for a larger bust so that it better conforms to the body. This dart can be steamed over the edge of a tailor's ham to preserve the curve.

4. Two or three very small darts in front and back on a skirt are prettier than one long dart, and will give less trouble in eliminating the points.

5. Darts should always be slit to within ½″ of point and pressed open in order to be as inconspicuous as possible (2).

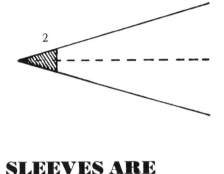

SLEEVES ARE KEYNOTES

While sleeves in themselves rarely make fashion news—the leg-o'-mutton inspiration happens about once a century—they are decidedly important to the overall look of your designer original. The fit and appearance of the sleeves definitely complete the picture. Basically, there are three types of sleeves—set-in, raglan and the kimono (plain or gusseted). Of the three, the most popular and comfortable is the set-in version. There are many variations in length and design that lend themselves particularly well to couture dressmaking (3–8).

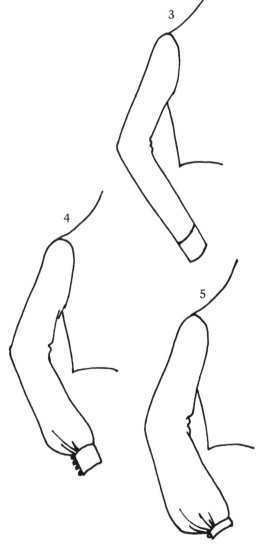

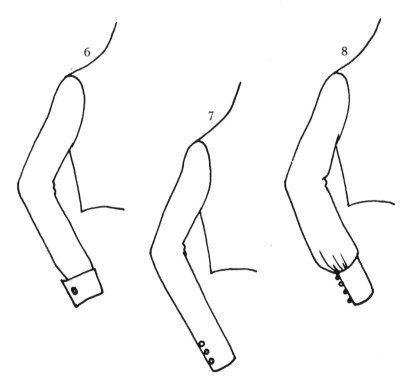

HOW TO SET IN SLEEVES_____

1. Ease-stitch the cap of sleeve between notches indicated on seam line. Place a second row of stitches ¼″ toward outer edge of cap. Leave thread ends on both sides of double row of stitches (9). Pull both threads together to ease cap of sleeve and wind thread around a pin until sleeve is set into armhole so that the ease can be adjusted to fit armhole (10). Baste seams. Try on for fit and width. Make any necessary adjustments. Then stitch seams and press open.

2. Couturiers set sleeves into a garment by placing sleeves and garment right side up. Match notches or cross marks. Turn in seam allowance on cap of sleeve and pin to sewing line of armhole with pins in opposite direction to the seam (11).

3. Pin sleeves all around and slip-baste with small stitches. Try on to see if sleeves hang properly, then turn on wrong side and machine-stitch.

4. For an alternate sleeve-setting technique, turn bodice wrong side out and place sleeve inside bodice, right sides together. Pin sleeve to armhole starting at shoulder seam and underarm seam. Match all notches. Check to see that ease is evenly distributed between notches and tie thread ends. Baste sleeve into dress at sewing line (try on for fit), then machine stitch (12).

5. To press cap of sleeve, use a tailor's ham or sleeve board. With sleeve turned wrong side out, place cap on edge of cushion and steam press with point of iron on sewing line and a scant ½″ beyond. From notch to notch underarm seams are pressed together with point of iron on sewing line.

THE RAGLAN SLEEVE_____

This basic sleeve variation has a diagonally fitted armhole, rather than the shaped curve of a set-in sleeve. A raglan sleeve is usually slit at the shoulder to achieve proper fit. Careful seaming and clipping of curves is necessary here in order to create a smooth-fitting shoulder and an armhole that doesn't pull (13).

1. Stitch the dart seam at the shoulder and press open. Stitch sleeve to back and front sides of gar-

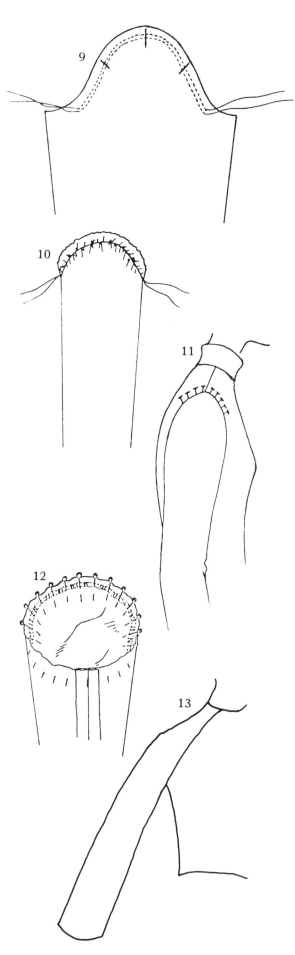

[49]

14   SHOULDER DART

RAGLAN SLEEVE

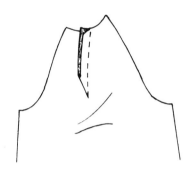

15   NOTCHING SEAMS

ment, carefully matching construction marks. Clip curves where necessary and press seams open (14).

2. Stitch garment and sleeve at underarm in one step. Press seam *up* at underarm (15).

TO FINISH A STRAIGHT SLEEVE

Place a bias fold of interfacing in the hemline of the sleeve, extending interfacing 1″ above fold line. Attach interfacing only to underlining with a basting stitch on the fold line. Turn up hem of sleeve and finish with seam binding (16).

TAILORED SLEEVE WITH LAPPED-BUTTON CLOSING

This type of sleeve is usually cut with a separate piece called an undersleeve. The seam of the sleeve should be in line with the small finger of your hand (17).

1. Underline the sleeve, baste and stitch. Clip the seam on underlap, ⅝″ above opening point, and press seam open from armhole to lap; press underlap forward.

2. Interface hemline and lap closing, extending interfacing 1″ beyond seam allowance.

3. Now stitch a seam binding on both sides of lap opening, close to edge. The under part of the lap is turned back close to seam binding. The upper part of the lap is turned back on the seam allowance line. Finish with a hemming stitch (18).

4. Align the lap closing and mark your buttons and loops. Hand-made thread loops or fabric loops make an attractive closing.

TAILORED SLEEVE

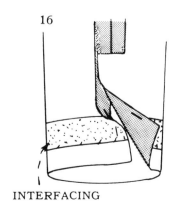

16

INTERFACING

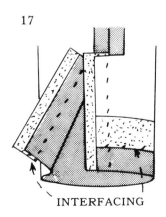

17

INTERFACING

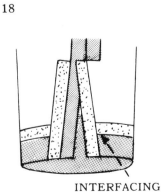

18

INTERFACING

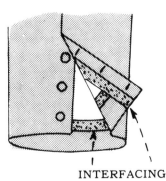

INTERFACING

SHIRTWAIST SLEEVE WITH BAND CUFF

1. Make a regular underarm seam. Place the underlining on the right side of your fabric and baste.

2. Mark a slash 2″ high, in line with the small finger of your hand, for an opening on the bottom of your sleeve. Run two machine stitches ¼″ apart coming to a point on top of the slash line (19). Cut in-between the two rows of stitches. Now turn the underlining to the wrong side. Baste and press slash. Re-baste the underlining onto the sleeve; baste and stitch the sleeve seam and press open.

3. If your sleeve is not underlined, face the slash with either self fabric or underlining fabric (20).

4. Make the band in one piece on the straight grain, extending it 1″ for the lap if you are making large bound buttonholes. Attach the interfacing on half the band only, but, if fabric is *not* heavy, interface entire band (21). Bound buttonholes should be made while the band is flat. On the wrong side, stitch both ends and turn band to right side. Finish buttonholes through band. If you are making small machine-made buttonholes, the band should be the same width as sleeve (22).

5. Shirr the back part of the sleeve on both sides of the slash. Attach the band, right sides together, starting at the front part of the slash. The band will extend beyond the sleeve for the lap for buttonholes. Baste and stitch the two ends. Press seam down. On the wrong side, turn under seam allowance and finish with a hemming stitch.

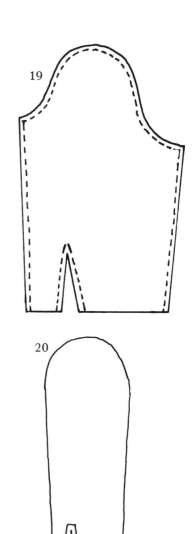

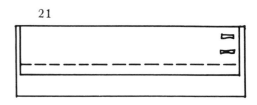

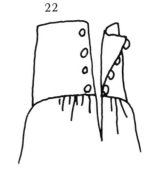

SHIRTSLEEVE THAT TURNS BACK ON ITS OWN BAND

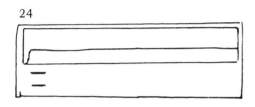

1. For this finish, the sleeve should be cut like the banded sleeve, with the length of the sleeve depending on the width of the cuff. Make buttonholes on the band section as you would for a sleeve with a band. Interface the entire cuff; then, right sides together, baste-stitch on the wrong side (23).

2. Turn to the right side and press. Attach to the sleeve as described above.

STRAIGHT BAND CUFF

1. Make a bias fold double the width of the cuff desired, plus ¾" seam allowance on each side for turning under the sleeve hem. Interface half of the cuff with bias Siri, extending the interfacing 1" beyond the fold line (24).

2. Stitch the seam and press. Turn cuff. Do not press fold line. Pipe the cut ends of cuff with seam binding or China silk; baste and sew cuff on inside of sleeve hem (25).

Couture Tip

■ You can also shape a straight, tight sleeve by making two small darts at the elbow to give the bending room required for comfort. On soft fabrics, a very small amount of ease or one small dart at elbow is sufficient.

NEAT NECKLINE TECHNIQUES

After hours and hours of work, the total couture effect of a new dress can be ruined by a neckline that is stretched, tight or just not right! Be sure you always win—by a neck—via the following methods:

ACHIEVE PERFECT SHAPE

1. A bias tape can be your best ally in shaping a neckline. This tape can be used to make a low oval neck, a V-neck, or any other shape you wish. It can also be utilized to correct the line of a curved seam. For a jewel or high, round neckline, place the tape around the neck, beginning at the center front. Pull it into the shape and curve you want. Pin well and firmly on one side only so that tape will not shift. The other side can be pinned here and there just to keep tape in place.

2. Remove the garment and with a chalk, mark the top edge of the tape on the neckline. Remove pins; be sure the line is smooth and not ragged. Run a basting stitch on the chalk line.

3. To transfer your new neckline marking to the opposite side, pin the neck together (matching center front, shoulder seams and back) and with a tracing paper and tracing wheel transfer the marking of the basted stitch to the other side of the neck.

4. If the neckline pulls, it may be necessary to clip it here and there to the stay stitch. Don't be afraid to clip as many times as necessary until your neckline lies smoothly.

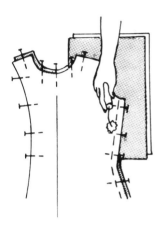

If you have fitted a good muslin on yourself, you won't be frustrated by a gaping neckline, bad shoulder lines or any other imperfections that may distort the neckline. They will have been corrected in the fitted muslin.

Incidentally, if your shoulders slope, this can have some effect on the neckline. It is better to build up the outer edge of the shoulder with a small pad than to try to fit it to the slope of the shoulder line. A straighter shoulder will make your entire garment hang better. It will also eliminate the fabric breaking over the bustline. By pulling up a fabric to conform to the slope in the shoulder you can easily distort the grain and cause problems in the body fit.

NECKLINE FINISHES_____

The appropriate neckline facing is always included with your dress pattern and is usually cut on the same grain as the garment proper. While details for a regular neckline facing are given under the section on facings in Chapter 7, below is a special neckline finish you may wish to perfect:

OUTSIDE FINISH SHAPED FACING____

1. For a yoke or collar effect, a facing brought to the outside of the garment can be effective. Stitch the front facing to the back facing at shoulder seams and trim. Clip and re-sew that area of shoulder seam that will be under the facing so that the seam will not show on the neck edge (26).

2. Pin the right side of the facing to the garment's

26

[53]

wrong side. Baste and stitch along neck edge; trim and clip seam.

3. Turn facing right side out and press. Turn in the free edge and baste, matching grains. Press. Complete the outside facing via top stitching or blind stitching to garment.

GUIDE TO COLLARS

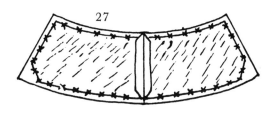

27

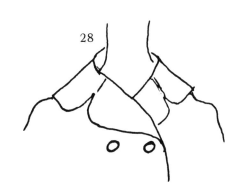

28

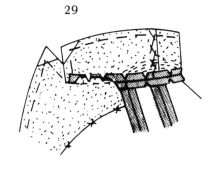

29

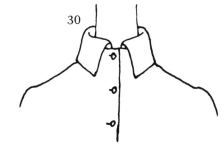

30

Collars are unquestionably a very important part of a garment, and probably the one unit that requires the most attention and tailoring. Collars depend a great deal on hand shaping to achieve the perfection expected of a couture garment.

Every collar should have some type of interfacing. For a shirt blouse or shirtwaist dress in lightweight fabric, a Siri interfacing is sufficient; if you're making a coat or suit, or a wool coat dress, a tailor's canvas should be used. Depending on the weight and type of material you are using, you will have to judge the weight of the interfacing required to give your collar a lovely, smooth, rolled shape.

Remember, the more you curve the collar, the flatter the collar will lie; if you want your collar to roll, it should be cut with very little or no shape.

FOR A TAILORED COLLAR

1. Cut the collar according to your pattern. Collars should be cut on the bias grain since this line molds better. The undercollar should be cut with a center back seam so that the grain is the same on both sides. It is the undercollar that gives the shape to the upper collar, since the interfacing is attached to this part of the collar. (Note: the upper collar pattern is usually slightly larger than the undercollar to allow for fabric taken up by the roll line [27-32].)

2. Seam the back of the collar; press seam open, then attach the interfacing. Don't lap the interfacing at the back seam. Cut it to meet and connect the seam with a catch stitch so it lies flat and smooth. Catch the interfacing to undercollar piece by hand with a long padding stitch that won't show on the right side of fabric. The padding stitches should be closer at the neck and roll line. Trim rounded edge to stitch line and notch. Cut back interfacing to seam line and cut across corners.

[54]

3. Shape the undercollar by placing it on a tailor's ham or soft pad. Use your hand and steam only to acquire a proper shape and a smooth roll. A thick cotton roll placed under the roll line and steamed may do the trick for you (33).

4. Place the upper collar over the undercollar and shape it on the tailor's ham. Start pinning at neck; be sure to leave sufficient fabric for the roll line so that the collar won't pucker. Pin toward outer edge and baste all around. Hold up the collar to see if you have achieved the roll line you want and if the collar lies smoothly without a break. (If you did not cut the upper collar slightly larger, you will find that the seam allowance on the upper collar is smaller than that of the undercollar. Don't be alarmed. This extra fabric was taken up in the roll of the collar.)

5. Mark the new seam line on the upper collar. Re-pin and re-baste, using the new seam line of the upper collar. Place the collar, right sides together; baste and stitch outside ends and curved edge. Leave open the section that will be attached to the neckline. Clip the rounded edges where necessary for a smooth roll. Turn to right side.

6. Using a needle or pin, pull out the rounded edge and corners of collar. Baste edge, pulling the seam slightly to underside so that the stitches do not show from the top. Steam the collar on the tailor's ham and flatten the seam a little with the palm of your hand or a pounding block. Re-shape the roll line a little; then remove basting. Now the collar is ready to be attached to your garment.

7. Pin and baste the undercollar right sides together to neckline of garment, starting at center back to finish line at front of neck or lapel. Stitch and press seam open. Stretch undercollar slightly when mounting.

8. The overcollar should be basted down, starting at center back, and attached to facings in front. Stitch only the area where collar and facings join. Press this seam open. The back of the overcollar should face down so that the lining can be sewn to it.

9. With a blind stitch, secure the front and back collar through the stitching line where facing and collar join.

[55]

31   ATTACH COLLAR
STARTING CENTER BACK

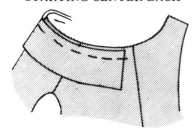

32   TURN FRONT FACING
OVER COLLAR

COLLAR   FACING

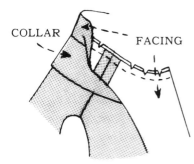

NOTCH NECKLINE

FACING TURNED TO INSIDE

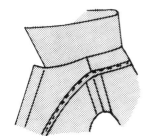

33

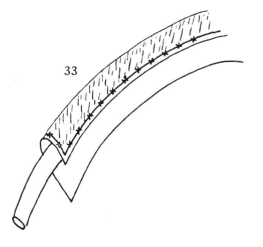

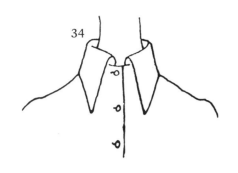

A SHIRTWAIST OR SHIRT COLLAR

1. Cut your undercollar and upper collar on the straight grain in one piece. Interface with a back seam. Baste and sew the outside edge and sides of collar. Turn to right side; using a pin or needle, pull out the corners of collar. Steam-press lightly (34).

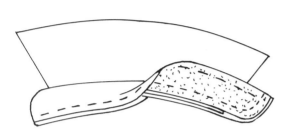

2. Stretching collar slightly, baste under part of neck of garment on the sewing line, starting at center back, matching all notches and cross marks. Then stitch together and press seam *up* if you are not going to put a facing on the back of the neck. A collar should never be eased to the neckline—it will cause the fabric to "break." Instead, by stretching the neckline just a little you can achieve a very good roll.

3. Place front facings right sides together. Collar will then be between the facing and front of garment. Baste. Stitch facing and collar on the sewing line of the neck. Press this seam *open* and turn back facing.

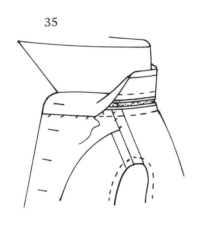

4. Baste top of collar, turning in seam allowance in back and checking to see if collar lies smoothly. Hand-finish with small stitches.

5. For a facing on the back of neck, press the seam open on undercollar, baste down top collar and stitch facing to neckline of top collar, right sides together.

6. Press *open*. Connect to front facing at shoulder.

FOR A SHIRT COLLAR WITH BAND NECK

1. Interface one side of the band. Attach neckline of the collar to sewing line of the band with right sides together. Baste. Place the other part of band, right sides together, on collar. Baste and stitch on sewing line, including the two ends. Collar will be encased between the band. Clip neckline (35).

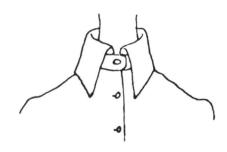

2. Starting at center back, place band, right sides together, on neckline of garment, matching center back, shoulder seam lines, notches or cross marks. Baste and stitch to neckline and sewing line of facing. Press seam *up*. Turn under seam allowance in back and finish with a hemming stitch.

[56]

FOR A TURTLENECK OR ROLLED COLLAR

1. Cut your band on bias grain, double the width of the collar, plus seam allowances. Attach bias interfacing of Siri or heavy Si Bonne on one-half of the collar, extending the interfacing about ¾″ beyond the fold line. If the fabric is thin you can interface the entire band (36, 37).

2. Fold the band in half and baste around the neckline of the garment to see if the band is the correct length. If you have to shorten it, mark the back. The band lends itself to a better fit if you stretch the mounting line as you attach it to the neckline. Try on the garment to be sure of the fit of the band and roll line.

3. Remove the band, make the necessary adjustments in length, turn to wrong side and stitch the two short ends. Press open and turn to right side.

4. Attach to neckline of garment, starting center front, right sides together, and pin and baste to center back.

5. Stitch and press seam *up*. Clip neckline. Finish the inside by turning under the seam allowance and hemming.

FOR A CLOSE-FITTING BAND COLLAR

1. This should be cut to shape. Cut a slightly curved strip of muslin and baste it to the neckline of your dress. Try it for shape and size. Make necessary corrections (38, 39).

2. If the muslin fits, cut two pieces from your muslin pattern, allowing for seams.

3. Interface, baste and stitch together on wrong side, leaving bottom open to be attached to neckline.

4. Starting at center front, attach to neckline with right sides together, matching center, back and side seams. Baste and stitch; clip and press seams *up*. Finish inside by turning under seam allowance and hemming.

FOR A SHAWL COLLAR

1. The interfacing should be applied to the under-shawl collar with padding stitches closer at fold line and catch stitches around edges (40).

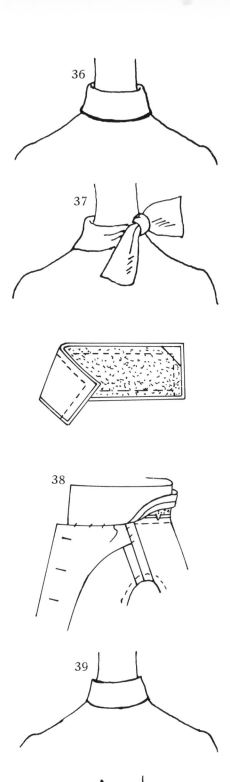

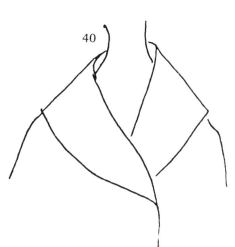

[57]

2. Baste and stitch upper collar to undercollar, right sides together, and turn. Baste outside edge of collar and steam.

3. Attach undercollar to mounting line of garment neck, matching center, back and side seams. Then catch upper collar to garment with a catch stitch so that lining can be mounted to it.

PERFECT POCKETS

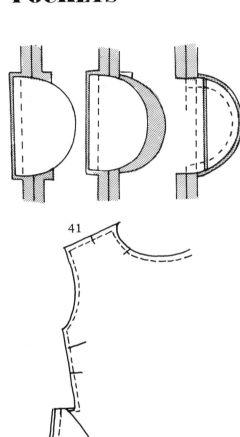

41

Pockets play an important role as a decorative and useful addition to a garment. They are varied as to design and type, but, with one exception, they all have one thing in common: they must be interfaced. The exception applies to seamed pockets whose role is solely utilitarian and behind-the-scenes—therefore, the softer the better.

The interfacing preserves the shape of the pocket as well as the wearing quality. Depending on the weight of the fabric and the firmness required, you must decide on the interfacing to use. In some fabrics, Siri is sufficient; in others, hair canvas is required.

Follow these techniques for pockets that are couture-perfect.

SEAMED POCKETS

1. Pockets placed in seams are very easy to make and should be worked into garment before the side seam is closed. Place pocket lining on garment extension of front seam, right sides together, and stitch across extension line. Repeat same on back side seam (41).

2. All tracing marks should be basted so that they show on right side of fabric.

3. Place back and front, right sides up, matching all seam lines, cross marks or notches. Pin together on sewing line with pins in opposite direction to seam.

4. Slip-baste with small stitches on right side, then turn inside out and stitch by machine on sewing line, the side seam and all around edge of pocket. Double-stitch the outside edge of pocket for extra strength.

5. Clip corners at the pocket extension so that seams can be pressed open and the pocket placed toward the front of the garment.

[58]

PATCH POCKETS (WITH SELF LINING)

1. Cut double fabric. Place the interfacing on the outer half. Baste the two pieces right sides together and stitch. Allow a small opening on the bottom for turning. Clip where necessary. Trim interfacing and corners and turn to right side (42).

2. Pull out seams and corners with a needle or pin and baste around the edge, turning slightly to underside (43).

3. Steam and use a pounding block for edge. Close opening with a slip stitch. Variations can be made on the basic patch pocket—adding a pleat, for instance (44).

PATCH POCKETS (WITH COMPLEMENTARY LINING)

1. Interface the outer fabric and trim. Turn down a 1½″ hem on top of pocket. Cut lining from edge of turned-down hem to bottom of pocket. Allow for a ½″ hem on top of lining (45).

2. Place hem of pocket over lining hem. Baste lining and pocket right sides together and stitch, starting at top of hem around bottom and up other side. Cut across corners and turn to right side (46).

3. Attach lining to hem facing with a slip stitch. Steam, using a pounding block.

FLAP POCKETS

This sportive addition to a garment should be made in the same manner as patch pockets, but one side must be left with a raw edge to be stitched to the garment, turned down and tacked ¼″ from the top on both ends. The back pocket should be cut on the same grain as the garment. The slash line should be indicated on the right side of fabric (47).

1. On right side, stitch the back pocket piece ⅛″ above slash line, allowing ends to extend 1″ on each side (48).

2. Cut a strip 1½″ wide and 1″ longer than slash line. Baste and sew on lower pocket mounting line which should be ⅛″ below slash line (49).

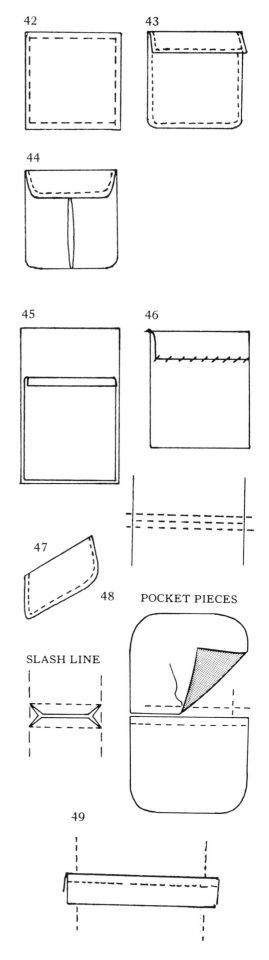

SLASH LINE

POCKET PIECES

[59]

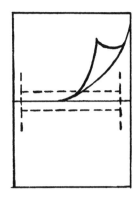

50

Baste front pocket piece on same sewing line and stitch. Front pocket piece should be cut in thin fabric (50).

3. On the inside of the garment cut through the slash line through the outer layer of fabric and diagonally to corners forming triangles ½" long at both ends (51).

4. Pull the pocket pieces through to the inside, back part of pocket facing down.

5. Stitch the triangles to the pocket pieces firmly on both ends. Lay garment on machine right side up; turn back to front, revealing triangles, and stitch triangles to strips firmly. Then stitch around the outer edges of the pocket (52).

WELT POCKETS

1. Mark your slash line. Then mark a mounting line ¼" above and ¼" below the slash line, just as you would for a bound buttonhole. Place an interfacing on wrong side of garment over pocket area to preserve the pocket line. Attach to underlining (53).

2. Make a strip on straight grain 1½" wide, 2" longer than slash line. Fold in half, right sides out, and stitch ¼" above the cut edge. Place the strip, cut edges together, on the lower pocket marking; baste and stitch on same stitching line (54).

51

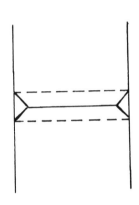

52

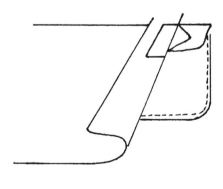

53

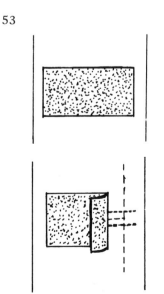

54

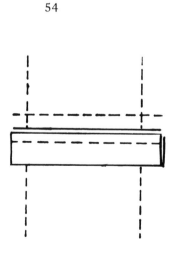

3. Place pocket piece with welt turned down on right side of lower mounting line. (Pocket will extend on both sides.) Baste and stitch on same stitching line (55).

4. The underpocket should be cut on same fabric grain as the garment. With the right side of pocket piece on upper mounting line, baste and stitch. Press seam open.

5. Cut through slash line in center between the two stitching lines, cutting the interfacing and underlining to within ½″ from ends; then cut to corners, forming triangles on each side. Turn the two pocket sections to inside through the slash line. The welt in the lower section should fill in the space between the mounting lines and lie flat.

6. Place the garment on machine, right side up, and turn back the front so that you can see the triangle. On wrong side, stitch through the triangles and pocket pieces. Then stitch all around pocket pieces. Steam and flatten with a pounding block.

BUTTONHOLE POCKET

1. Mark pocket line as you would for a bound buttonhole (see next section). Indicate the slash line and a mounting line ¼″ above and ¼″ below slash line (56).

2. Make two strips 1″ wide and 1″ longer than the slash line. Fold in half, right side out. Mark middle of each strip and place middle of each strip on the two guidelines, cut edges toward slash line, and baste (57).

3. Place the upper pocket piece on lower stitching line of welt and underpocket piece on upper stitching line of welt. Baste and stitch both through all thicknesses. Cut through the slash line to within ⅝″ from ends and then to corners, forming triangles (58).

4. Pull pocket pieces through to wrong side. Your two strips will meet in the center. Place on the machine right side up. Turn back the front, revealing the triangles, and stitch the triangles through the strips at both ends. Stitch all around the pocket pieces and steam the welt.

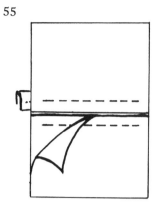

55

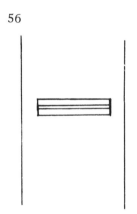

56

57

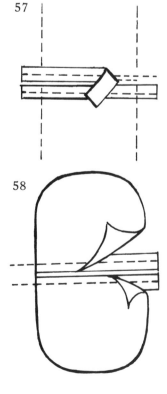

58

[61]

BUTTONHOLE BASICS

Aside from fabric, design and fit, there is one small but important detail that spells the difference between couture and sew-and-go fashions: the type of buttonholes used. The hurry-up sewer opts for machine-made buttonholes; but the woman with patience and know-how to make the bound, couture variety, will in the long run produce a much finer-looking outfit—only if solely on the basis of these vital additions.

If you've been thinking you can never learn to make a professional buttonhole, put your worries aside and take out some scrap fabric. Practice makes perfect, and if you follow these directions, you'll have bound buttonholes under very nice control.

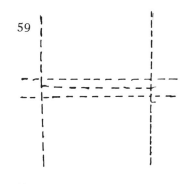

1. When you traced your garment originally, the buttonhole marks would have been indicated on the underlining. Now, trace with a small basting stitch all buttonhole lines on the right side of the fabric. Indicate these with double lines ¼″ apart. Extend these lines ¼″ longer on both sides. Mark with a vertical line and ruler the actual end of the slash line and sewing line. (This should be ¼″ in from both ends of the buttonhole. Your slash line will be the center of your double buttonhole lines [59].)

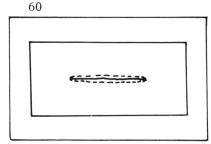

2. All buttonholes should be ¼″ longer than the size of the button to be used. (Determine exact size by slashing a scrap of fabric and pushing through a button.)

3. If your fabric ravels easily, press a small piece of Armo onto the wrong side of fabric under the underlining so you won't lose your markings (60).

4. Prepare a strip of fabric, cut on the straight grain, 1½″ wide and 1″ longer than buttonholes. Fold in half, right side out, and machine stitch ⅛″ in from fold edge. Insert a thin buttonhole cord before stitching (61).

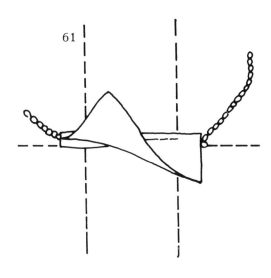

5. Cut one side of the folded strip close to stitching line. Place the folded strip on one of the double guidelines, with cut side on right side of fabric. Check to see if strip is centered on guideline.

6. Then baste and stitch through same stitching line that you have on folded strip. Stitch only to vertical lines.

[62]

7. Sew on the second strip on guideline. Ends will extend ½″ beyond vertical stop lines. Repeat for all buttonholes.

8. On wrong side of garment, cut through underlining, interfacing and outer fabric to within ¼″ from slash line at both ends; then diagonally to corners, forming a triangle. Be careful not to cut into finishing strip. Turn the two finishing strips inside until the folded edges meet in the center of the buttonhole. On the right side of garment turn back the two triangular edges so that you can stitch the triangles firmly to the finishing strips (62).

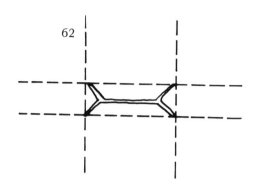

9. Turn back the facing and, with pins at each end of slash line, indicate slash line on facing (63).

10. Baste a bias strip of organza or thin Si Bonne over slash line on right side of facing and stitch all around close to slash line, leaving just enough space between to cut the slash line (64).

11. Cut slash line and turn organza inside and press. This will give you a clean finish around buttonhole.

12. Turn back facing and sew all around buttonhole with a small hand stitch.

Couture Tips on Buttonholes

■ For heavy wool garments a hand-made buttonhole using a heavy buttonhole twist is often used in place of a bound buttonhole.

■ For shirts and shirtwaist dresses in thin fabric, a hand-made buttonhole can be substituted, using a buttonhole-twist thread. If there are many buttonholes on a garment, a machine-worked French buttonhole is very practical.

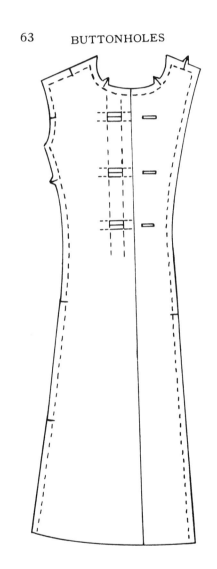

63   BUTTONHOLES

■ Buttonholes should be placed no less than ⅝″ to ¾″ from fold line and, for coats, the width should be at least 1″. The top buttonhole should be placed so that the top of the button should be ½″ below the close line of the neck. The bottom buttonhole should be about 5″ above the hemline.

■ Always indicate top and bottom buttonholes first; then divide the space between for the balance of button placement. If your garment is belted, try to avoid placing a button under the belt.

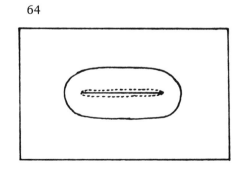

■ Buttons should always be centered on a garment.

ZIPPER TIPS

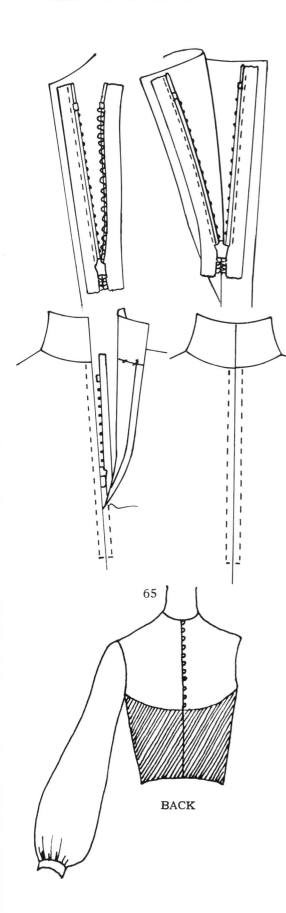

65

BACK

There are several different ways of setting in a zipper, depending on the design of the garment, the fabric, etc. For a basic dress, with an opening in the center back, this method works best:

1. Since a zipper is put on last in couture apparel, your neck facing has already been attached. Open out facing and turn opening edges toward wrong side of garment along seam lines. Baste turned-in facing and seam lines the length of the zipper. Press.

2. Open zipper and pin into folded edge of closing 1/4" down from finished neckline. Center of zipper should be even with fold edge. Repeat on opposite side. Trim excess tape at neck edge if necessary.

3. Test positioning of zipper by closing—it must lie smoothly. Baste; then remove pins.

4. Sew with a hand-picked stitch 1/4" from edge.

5. Turn facing down into place, turn in zipper edge of facing slightly in order to clear teeth. Slip-stitch in place.

THE INVISIBLE ZIPPER

In this method the zipper is machine sewn into a garment.

1. Press the zipper tape before beginning. Start the zipper about 1/2" down from the waistband if making pants or a skirt and 1/2" from the neckline for a dress.

2. Open the zipper and place face down on right side of fabric with the tape toward cut edge of seam allowance. Baste into place. Stitch with a zipper foot close to the teeth, starting at the top, down to the slider. Fasten stitch securely.

3. Place other side of zipper on opposite side of opening. Close zipper to see if you are aligned correctly. If so, open zipper and baste. Then stitch close to teeth. Secure lower end of zipper to seam allowance by hand.

4. Turn back tape and seam allowance and catch both to underlining with a hemming stitch.

Couture Tips

■ When putting a zipper in a chiffon dress, run the zipper only to the point where the nude yoke begins.

The opening from that point to the neckline can be piped in chiffon and closed with hand thread loops and self-covered buttons size 22 or 24 (65). The buttons can also be grouped three at the neck, three in the center and three where the yoke meets the zipper. Use a chiffon zipper so that the dress will not bulge.

1. Hems should be marked from the floor *up*. Don't stand on carpeting when taking a length.

2. After taking an even length all around, the back should be dropped ¼″ to nothing at side seams.

3. Mark the fold line of the hem with a basting stitch and finish raw edge with seam binding. All hems, including sleeves, should be finished with binding so that press marks won't show on fabric. Facings where possible should also be finished with seam binding. An alternate approach is to turn up a very small hem, double-stitch the edge and cut close before pressing.

4. When finishing a hem, neckline, sleeve or facing in a dress, jacket or coat, make a bias strip of Siri or Si Bonne about 1½″ to 2″ wide. Fold in half and baste the center of the strip onto the fold line of the fabric so that the stitches don't show on the right side of fabric. Then turn up hem and baste ½″ from fold line. Pin and baste top of hem and blind-stitch, catching only the underlining. This will give your finished edge a soft rounded look as in couture clothes instead of a hard, flat look.

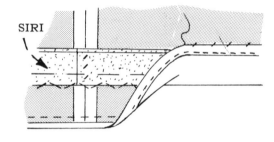

SIRI

5. Steam lightly, without placing the iron on the folded edge.

Couture Tips

■ If you are making an A-line skirt, you will find that the hem forms pleats when you turn it up. To eliminate this extra fullness run a machine stitch on the cut edge and pull the thread so that the hem conforms with the garment. Then press with a steam iron to shrink away as much of the fullness as possible. The seam binding should be sewn on *after* you have pressed away the fullness (66).

■ Always hang a chiffon or jersey dress for a day or two before taking a length. The fabric has a tendency to stretch, especially on the bias grain. Allow a

66

little extra length for chiffon as your dress will "jump up" after stitching the hem.

■ With chiffon and other sheer fabrics, determine the length, allowing ¾" for hand rolling. (Place the chiffon over tissue paper when stitching.) Run a machine stitch on the edge of your hem marking. Then cut evenly, close to the stitch. Roll edge a few inches at a time between thumb and forefinger and hem by hand, catching a single thread for each stitch.

■ Another very popular method of making a hem on chiffon is to determine the length and mark same all around with chalk or a basting stitch. Run a machine stitch on this mark, placing tissue paper under the chiffon on the machine. Then turn up the hem (it doesn't matter how uneven the turned-up hem is so long as your mark is even.) on the stitching line. Run a double machine stitch very close together on the very edge of the fold line. Press and trim all excess fabric close to the stitching line.

■ In hemming a knit fabric, since it has not been underlined, it's advisable to run a loose blind stitch halfway up the hem and a catch stitch at the top of hem. This will alleviate pull on the knit. You can also run a double machine stitch at the top of the hem; cut close to the stitching line or finish hem with a stretch-lace seam binding.

FLOURISHES WITH RUFFLES

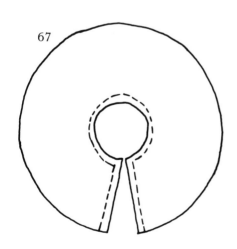

Ruffles are delightfully feminine and can add a definite designer cachet to a party-going dress. Here's how to perfect them:

CIRCULAR RUFFLES

1. The best way to cut circular ruffles is to make a paper pattern the size of the ruffle you want (67). Place heavy paper on your cutting board and secure it with push pins. On one end of a cord, make a loop and place a push pin through the loop and fasten it to the paper and cutting board.

2. Tie the other end of the cord around a marking pencil the width of the ruffle desired (allow for seams). Draw a complete circle, as you would with a compass, holding the pencil straight.

3. Then shorten the cord and draw a small circle in the center the same way. Remove pins and cut outer edge and inner circle. To make a very full ruffle the center circle should be small. The larger the center circle, the less full the ruffle. The circumference of the inner circle should be equivalent to the length of the area to which it will be applied.

4. Place this paper pattern on your fabric and mark the outer edge and inner circle with a pencil. Shift the pattern for as many circles as you require and mark. Then cut. Cut through each circle on the straight grain and join all the circles together. Press the seams open and trim. If your fabric is thin, cut double the quantity. Join the upper-layer and under-layer seams separately. Baste and stitch both outside edges together. Press on wrong side. Trim close to stitching line and press seams together. Turn to right side; baste the edge and press lightly.

5. If you want to hand-roll the hem edge (which requires a great deal of hand sewing, but achieves a very professional finish), run a machine stitch about ⅜″ from the edge and turn in a double narrow hem. Finish with a hemming stitch (68).

6. Another method of finishing an edge is to run a machine stitch ½″ from the edge. Turn under a ⅝″ hem. Run another machine stitch very close to the fold edge of hem and trim close to stitching line. This will give you a hem about ⅛″ wide (69).

7. The edge of a ruffle can also be finished with piping or binding.

8. Baste and sew the ruffle, placing cut edge along cut edge of the garment.

9. Face according to directions, later in this section, under HOW TO ATTACH RUFFLES.

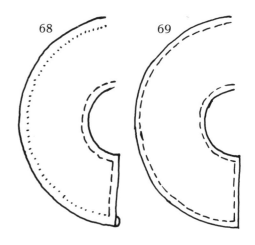

SHIRRED RUFFLES

1. A shirred ruffle should always be cut on the bias grain for graceful roll. Cut the strips double the desired width of the ruffle; allow for seams to be joined to the garment. Incidentally, 3″ of shirring are usually allowed per 1″ finish in a full ruffle; the ratio is two to one for less fullness. If fabric is firm, two to one is sufficient; thin fabrics require a three to one ratio.

2. Join all strips on the bias grain until you have sufficient length for your trim. If fabric is thin, underline with bias organza.

3. Fold fabric in half; don't press the fold line. Run a loose double machine stitch ¼″ from edge, leaving threads on both ends for pulling. Adjust the gathers for the length required.

4. Finish ruffle by inserting the shirred edge between the garment and facing as described below, or finish with a binding if ruffle is to be detachable.

LACE RUFFLES

1. Lace ruffles have many uses and can be employed in various ways to either trim a garment or create a design in themselves (70–76). Lace with a straight edge can be shirred by pulling a thread of the lace on the straight edge.

2. If the lace is scalloped on both edges it will have to be shirred by hand or machine.

HOW TO ATTACH RUFFLES

1. Baste and stitch ruffle to right side of garment, cut edges together. Place your facing right side on ruffle. Ruffle will be between garment and facing. Stitch on the same sewing line as the ruffle. Turn back facing; baste along the sewing line and finish the cut edge with seam binding and attach to underlining.

2. Ruffles can also be finished separately and sewed to garment with a slip stitch. The cut edge would then be finished with a binding of self fabric about ⅜″ wide.

3. If ruffle is made of washable fabric such as organdy, it should be made detachable and simply basted into garment.

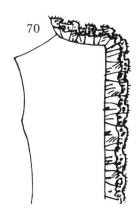
70

[68]

Expert Tailoring: Designer Techniques

XII

NOW it's time to put your new-found expertise to the test. Your machine is threaded, bobbin in place, and ironing board and steam iron standing by for action: you wouldn't dare skip the important step of pre-pressing each unit of a garment as it is stitched, would you?

This chapter will take you from the basic procedures for making a couture dress, through the methods for sewing skirts, pants, shirts and blouses, and will culminate in the *pièce de résistance* of any creative sewer: tailoring a coat or suit.

1. Run a stay stitch around neck, armhole and shoulder about ½″ from edge. This is a "holding" stitch to prevent stretching while working on the garment (1). Baste and stitch your darts. Cut to within ¾″ from point and press open. Incidentally, side darts if used should be as short as possible so they won't show over the bosom.

2. Lay the front and side panel or back, right side up, on the table and pin the two units together. Turn under one seam allowance and place it on opposite seam allowance. It is important to reiterate the necessity of matching all construction lines, cross marks and darts. Pins should be at right angles to the seams. Slip-baste with small stitches and repeat until you have all units put together and basted.

3. Sleeves may be basted, but don't set in until garment is completely stitched. If you have a waistline, baste the skirt and waist together before proceeding. Try on garment to see if you need any altera-

STEP-BY-STEP PROCEDURE FOR A COUTURE DRESS

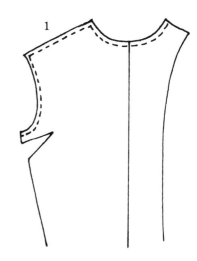

SHIRTWAIST DRESS

COLLAR

INTERFACING

FACING

INTERFACING

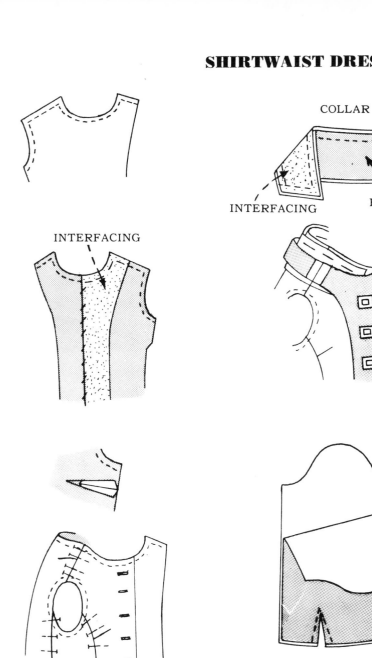

SLEEVE

FLAP POCKET

INTERFACING

FACING

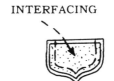

SIRI

PRINCESS DRESS

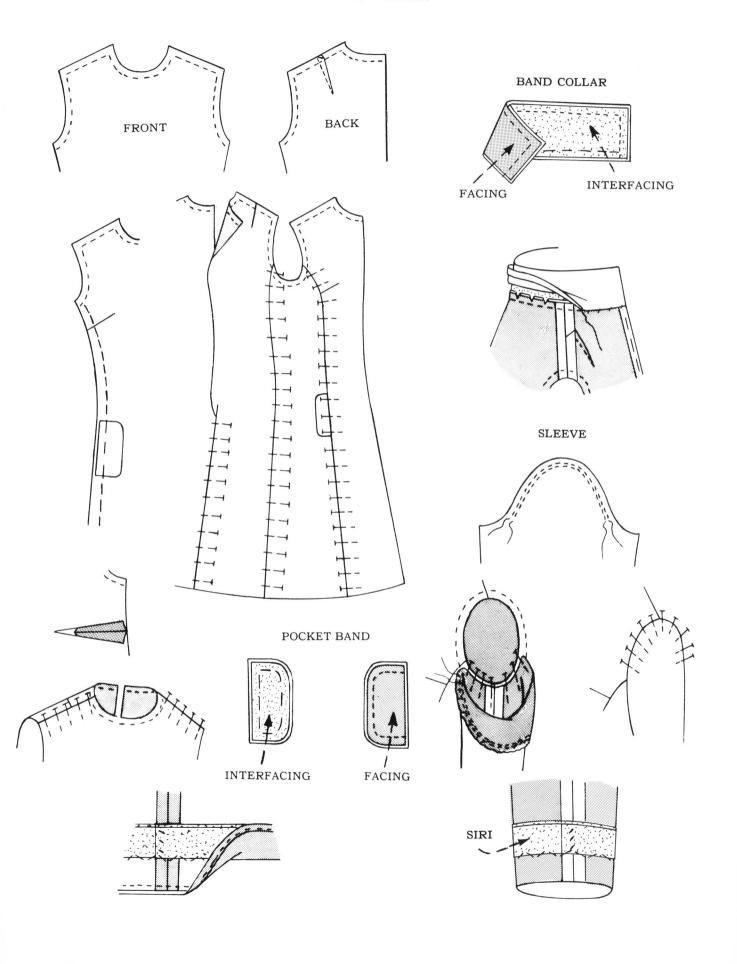

FRONT

BACK

BAND COLLAR

FACING

INTERFACING

SLEEVE

POCKET BAND

INTERFACING

FACING

SIRI

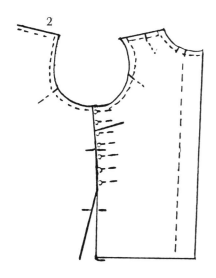

tions in the fit. (Keep your fingers crossed that you won't—chances are that you will!)

4. If so, place pins carefully, fitting one side only, but make sure you aren't pulling center grain line which should remain basted until garment is finished. Indicate alterations with a chalk pencil over the pins to mark the new sewing line. Remove pins and straighten new line. Then run basting stitch through to the underlining (2).

5. In order to transfer alteration lines to the other side of the garment, remove whatever basting stitches are necessary in order for fabric to lay flat and place right and left units together so you can transfer your new markings accurately. Place tracing paper, carbon side toward fabric, and run tracing wheel over new sewing line. Be sure both sides are pinned together *perfectly* so the new tracing marks will be the same on each side. This is the *only* accurate method for making both sides alike.

6. Here's where the game of patience vis-à-vis sewing comes into play. *Re-pin* and *re-baste* garment and try it on again to be sure the alteration has been correctly made before stitching.

7. If you have a waistline seam, separate waist from skirt and stitch separately. It's easier for handling and pressing. (Remember, as each unit is stitched, the seam should be pressed.)

8. After alterations have been made, the next step is a neckline facing. The appropriate facing is always included with your dress pattern. For a dress *with* sleeves, a separate neckline facing is indicated. Cut the required facing, stitch the shoulder seam and press open. Place the facing, right sides together, on the neckline of the dress; baste and stitch on the sewing line of neck.

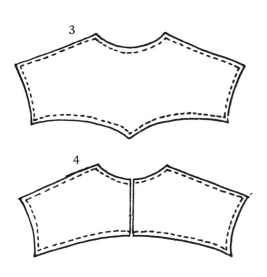

9. For a sleeveless dress, *without* buttonholes or collar, the armhole and neckline facing can be cut in one piece (3, 4). (Don't sew side seams of dress until facing is in.) Stitch shoulder seams of facing and press open; baste facing into armhole and neck, right sides together, then stitch and turn. Now you're ready to stitch side seams.

10. If you are making a shirtwaist dress or coat dress, to add interfacings, cut two strips of canvas or Siri the same width and shape as the facing. Pin

and baste this into the fold line. If cut properly, the facing will extend into the neckline and shoulder in front. Position your interfacing and attach to the garment with a zigzag stitch (5).

11. For easier handling, make buttonholes while garment is open. (Note: buttonhole markings should all be transferred to the outer fabric as per earlier instructions.)

12. Construct the collar as described on page 56 and attach to garment. If you're making a shirt-waist dress, run a basting stitch on the extension fold line so that it shows through on the right side of the fabric.

13. Set in sleeves.

14. Attach waist to skirt.

15. If the dress has a zipper, it's added as the last step in completing your garment.

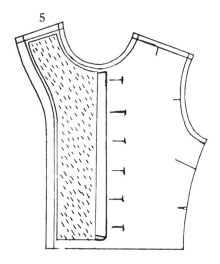

Couture Tips on Making Dresses

■ If fabric ravels, overcast seams by hand or run a double machine stitch on edge. There are machines today with attachments for overcasting seams—this eliminates hand work.

■ A roller foot is ideal for preventing seam puckering in such fabrics as Qiana. Synthetics and knits should also be sewn with a roller foot to prevent cutting into the fibers. (For the latter, polyester thread is suggested, since it gives with the stretch of the knit. Don't use too tight a stitch.)

■ In making alterations, remember a garment should never be fitted tightly to the body. Sufficient ease should be allowed for appearance and comfort.

■ A raised waist has a younger look than a normal waistline. A dress without a cut-through waistline is adaptable to placement of belts. The soft ease generated by the belt is flattering to the figure.

■ When working with chiffon or lace, place a piece of tissue paper between the machine and the fabric when stitching. The tissue tears away easily and your fabric will not pull or pucker.

■ For chiffon, make the underbodice of crepe with a nude marquisette yoke. This avoids shoulder straps and helps to conceal heavy, dark seams. It also makes the dress hang better (6).

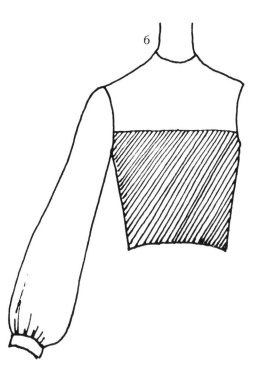

[75]

SKIRT THE ISSUE

Think of the importance of skirts. Never have they been as accepted as a major reflection of fashion. Today, all women from chic sophisticate to hip "flower-child" rely on this versatile fashion.

For women who sew at home, skirts present endless possibilities. They can be long or short, day or evening, sport or beachwear—all depending on the choice of fabric and where or how a skirt is worn. From the sewing standpoint, skirts are the least expensive clothing item to make. Each takes very little fabric, so you can afford to choose the finest and most exciting. You could never find ready-to-wear skirts for the price equal to making one yourself. Furthermore, think of the fun in choosing and combining fabrics and colors.

Skirts seldom deviate from the basic shapes. They may be longer or shorter, but the dictates of fashion don't change them to any great extent. In short, a great part of your wardrobe can be built around skirts. They are here to stay!

Unless you are choosing a fabric that requires special matching for the top, you will usually be able to find a simple sweater or shirt in matte jersey or synthetic knit in the stores. Remember, you don't have to match—just mix.

SUGGESTED SKIRT VARIATIONS

FOR BEACHWEAR: long skirt, slit in front with tie belt attached. Print or solid cotton or synthetic jersey (7).

FOR STREET OR SPORT: short or midi, to be worn over hot pants or tight-knit jumpsuit (8). Slit, wrapped or buttoned (9). Straight or slightly A-line (10). If you aren't the jumpsuit type, a sweater top provides equal chic, worn inside with a novelty belt, or as an overblouse accessorized with belt made of skirt fabric. Other tops: tailored shirts in crepe, jersey or synthetic knit; lightweight wool or challis. One of the smartest looks on the scene is a soft shirt, tucked inside the waist and belted.

FOR EVENING: can you measure the chic of a long black crepe or wool evening skirt with a simple black matte jersey sweater top, long black sleeves

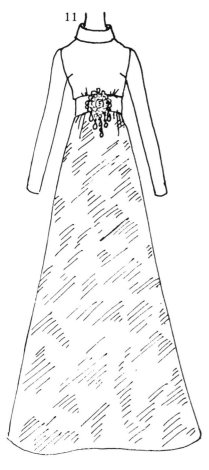

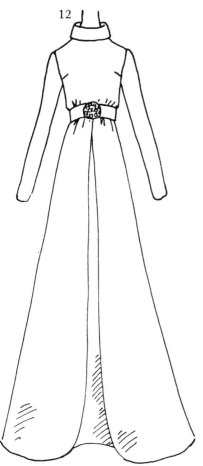

worn with a 2″ or 3″ wide jeweled belt of rhinestones or colored jewels (11)? An alternative would be a patent-leather belt with a large rhinestone or gold buckle. If your favorite jewelry is gold, by all means, opt for the gold buckle. Other effective fabrics for an evening skirt are matte jerseys, in prints or solids. Try to combine colors—this is more exciting than a head-to-toe solid look for evening. You can always pick up a third color for the belt.

Twin fabrics can also be dramatic: crepe with chiffon or organza in print or solid...velvet with matte jersey...brocade with matte jersey...lace with crepe or chiffon.

Evening skirts can be slit and worn over a contrasting color slip (12). Evening skirts should be soft, with a little ease around the waist, achieved either by shirring, or gentle pleats or darts (13).

STEP-BY-STEP TO A COUTURE SKIRT

Follow the same procedure as you would for a dress; cut the underlining and outer fabric, transferring all construction markings to each. Baste and try on to check fit before sewing.

1. Proceed in this manner. Stitch the darts and seams on the underlining and outer fabric separately. Then press the seams open.

2. Place the underlining and outer fabric, wrong sides together, and pin along the seams. Turn back the underlining and run a permanent basting stitch on the seam allowance to secure the lining.

3. Pin all outer edges, baste and run a machine stitch all around. Be sure the underlining lies smoothly on the outer fabric.

4. If you are making buttonholes in the skirt, this should be done before you turn back the facing. Place a strip of Siri the same width as the facing and extending 1″ beyond the fold line. Secure to fold line with a blind stitch. Finish your buttonholes through the facing and then you will be ready to attach the waistband.

5. Cut the waistband along the selvage edge or length grain of the fabric. (For a slimmer-looking

waistline when making a skirt with a heavy fabric, face the back of the waistband with taffeta; band must then be interfaced with tailor's canvas.) Place the interfacing to the fold line on the side of the band that is worn toward the inside. Secure interfacing to the fabric with a machine stitch on bottom and small ends. Attach the band to the skirt, right sides together, matching center front and side seam markings. Baste and stitch, including ends. Press seam *up*; pull out ends at the corners.

6. Run a basting stitch at the fold line of the band. Turn under seam allowance at the waist and hem. Press with steam; finish with hooks and eyes.

7. To determine the length of your garment, it's better to have someone help you so that you can be sure of an even length all around. Be sure to stand on a hard floor—not a rug. Mark the length with a skirtmarker or yardstick, using pins or chalk.

8. Indicate the fold line of the hem with a basting stitch to show on right and wrong sides. Cut a bias strip of firm Siri 3″ wide. Fold in half and, using a blind stitch, baste the folded edge of the strip to the fold line of the hem.

9. Turn up the hem, matching seams, and place pins at right angles to the folded hem. Baste the folded edge and remove pins. Sew a seam binding on cut edge of hem and baste all around. Finish hem with a slip stitch.

10. The facing of the skirt can be finished with the same seam binding or a piping of the underlining.

HOW TO MAKE PLEATED SKIRTS ___

For a machine-pleated skirt:

1. If the fabric is lightweight it should be underlined before it is sent out to be pleated. Use a China silk or lightweight Si Bonne for the underlining. Turn up the hem and finish with seam binding. If any adjustments have to be made in the length they will be made from the *top* after the pleating is done.

2. Pleats should hang straight, and since the waist measurements are smaller than the measurements of the width at the bottom of the skirt, you have to

13

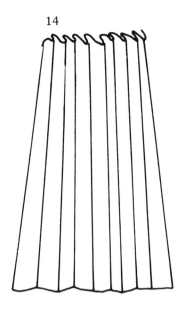

14

lap the top pleats until they conform to the waist measurements (14).

3. These pleats may need more overlap across the hips than they do in front or back, depending on your particular figure. Baste the pleats on top and attach a temporary waistband of ribbon or grosgrain. You can then adjust the pleats better, according to how they hang on you.

4. If you have a dress form this is the best way to fit the skirt. After all, the important factor in a pleated skirt is for the pleats to hang evenly. You may have to pull up the under part of the pleat or drop the outer fold. If the pleat swings away you must pull up the outer fold. If it laps over the next pleat you have to lift the underneath part. These adjustments are especially important when you are making wider pleats or unpressed pleats.

To make your own pleats, follow this method:

1. An unpressed pleated-skirt pattern will usually include all the necessary markings for the pleats. If, however, you are not using a pattern, do your own marking, via this system: Pin one pleat the width you want. Take the measurements of this pleat, starting where the pleat begins, to the fold line, under the fold line to the crease and then back to the fold line. Mark these measurements on hard paper. At each measurement on your paper pattern, draw a horizontal line so that you can easily see how to mark your fabric. Use this measurement as a guide, repeating in turn until you have marked the entire skirt (15).

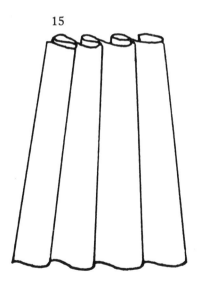

15

2. Follow the same principle as you would for a machine-pleated skirt. Baste across the top, lap the top pleats to conform to waist measurements. Place the skirt on a dress form to ascertain if the pleats are hanging evenly. Then proceed to stitch the seams and attach the waistband, as outlined above.

PANTS ARE CONTEMPORARY

It is definitely better—when making a pair of pants—to cut them first in muslin. Baste together and try them on for a fitting. Make all the necessary alterations on the muslin and mark all changes clearly in red chalk. The result will be a perfectly fitting pattern that will make the second and subsequent

pairs of pants much easier to sew—all you'll have to do is whip out your pattern and proceed.

STEP-BY-STEP TO COUTURE PANTS

1. After you have altered your muslin, place the muslin pattern on the fabric. Trace all construction markings with a tracing paper and tracing wheel to the wrong side of the outer fabric. Then outline all the markings with a small basting stitch so that they appear on the right side of the fabric. (Pants are usually unlined.)

2. Stitch the darts and press open. Pin together, right sides up, all seams and slip-baste. Try on again to be sure you don't need additional alterations. Stitch the seams and press open (16).

3. Putting in the zipper is the next step. The invisible machine-sewn zipper is best for pants. Press the tape on the zipper before applying. Start the zipper ½" from the waistline. Open the zipper and place it face down on right side of fabric with tape toward cut edge of fabric. Baste into place and stitch with a zipper foot close to the teeth, starting at the top and finishing at the slider. Fasten the thread by knotting.

4. Place the other side of the zipper on the opposite side of the opening. Close the zipper to see if you are aligned correctly. If you are, open the zipper, baste and stitch close to the teeth. Secure lower end of zipper by hand to seam allowance. Turn back tape and seam allowance and finish by hand with a blind stitch which does not show on the right side of fabric.

5. Now you are ready to make the waistband. If possible, the band should be cut on the lengthwise grain of the fabric, along the selvage edge. The interfacing should be basted into fold line of the band with a blind stitch to secure it. Stitch the bottom and the small ends by machine, and turn the band over to the right side. Press lightly .

6. Matching side markings and center-back markings, place the outside of the band, right sides together, on the sewing line of the waist. Baste and stitch; then press seam *up.* Turn in seam allowance on the inside of the band and hem to waistline. Fin-

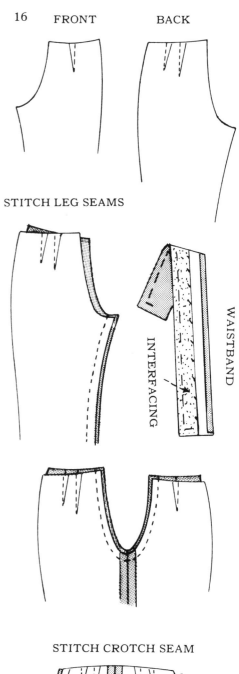

16 FRONT BACK

STITCH LEG SEAMS

INTERFACING

WAISTBAND

STITCH CROTCH SEAM

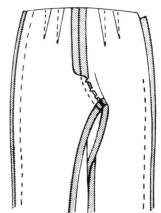

SHIRTS, BLOUSES COMPLETE THE PICTURE

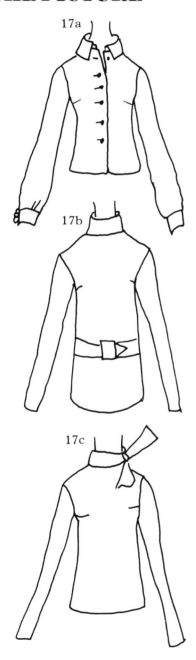

17a

17b

17c

No skirt or pants are complete without a complementary blouse, shirt or sweater-type top. While it is possible to choose from a wide variety of ready-to-wear selections, often you can come up with just the right mate for your skirt or pants if you do-it-yourself (17A, 17B, 17C). Since shirts and blouses do not require underlining, they are easy and rewarding to make. Here's how:

STEP-BY-STEP TO A COUTURE BLOUSE

1. Mark your fabric directly from the pattern, observing all construction marks and buttonhole placement markings. These should be transferred to the right side of the fabric with a basting stitch. (Interfacings are necessary only for collars, cuffs and facings.)

2. Sew the darts and press. Then sew side seams. Lay a strip of Siri or Si Bonne in the facing fold. Now put in your buttonholes. Shirts are most often made with French machine buttonholes. They can also be made by hand with a buttonhole stitch and buttonhole thread.

3. If you are making a shirt collar, interface it with Siri or Si Bonne. Stitch to sewing line of neck with the collar right sides together. Turn right side out and press. Mount the collar on the sewing line of your neck, starting at the center back to finish line in front. If collar goes into facing it should be stitched between the front of blouse and the facing. Then the facing is turned back. Turn up seam allowance on inside of neckline and finish with a hemming stitch.

4. Sew the seam on each sleeve and press. Slit the back of the sleeve 2″ up and either face the slit with self fabric or pipe. Shirr on either side of the slit.

5. Make the cuff or band as you did the collar (complete directions on page 56), interfacing similarly.

[82]

Make the buttonholes; then stitch all around, leaving one side open to attach to sleeve.

6. Sew on the band starting at the upper part of the slit and finishing at the under part.

Couture Tips

▪ For a turtleneck or rolled collar, cut a bias strip double the width plus seam allowance. Underline with a lightweight Si Bonne. Fold in half and attach to neckline of blouse starting at center front (18). Finish on wrong side, turn up seam allowance and hem. (For complete instructions, see page 57.)

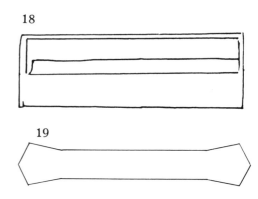

▪ If you are making a band collar that ties on the side, cut the bias strip long enough and double the width; widen at the ends for the tie. Underline with lightweight Si Bonne. Clean finish the entire strip except the area that attaches to neck from center back to side front. Stitch by machine and turn to right side. Attach to neckline of blouse starting at center back to side front. The rest of the band is attached to the neckline with snaps (19).

SHIRTWAIST BLOUSE

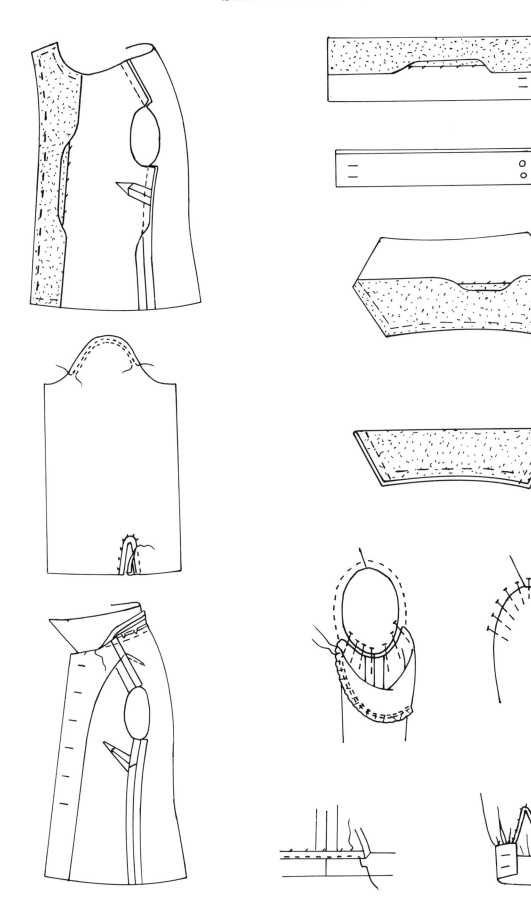

BAND COLLAR BLOUSE

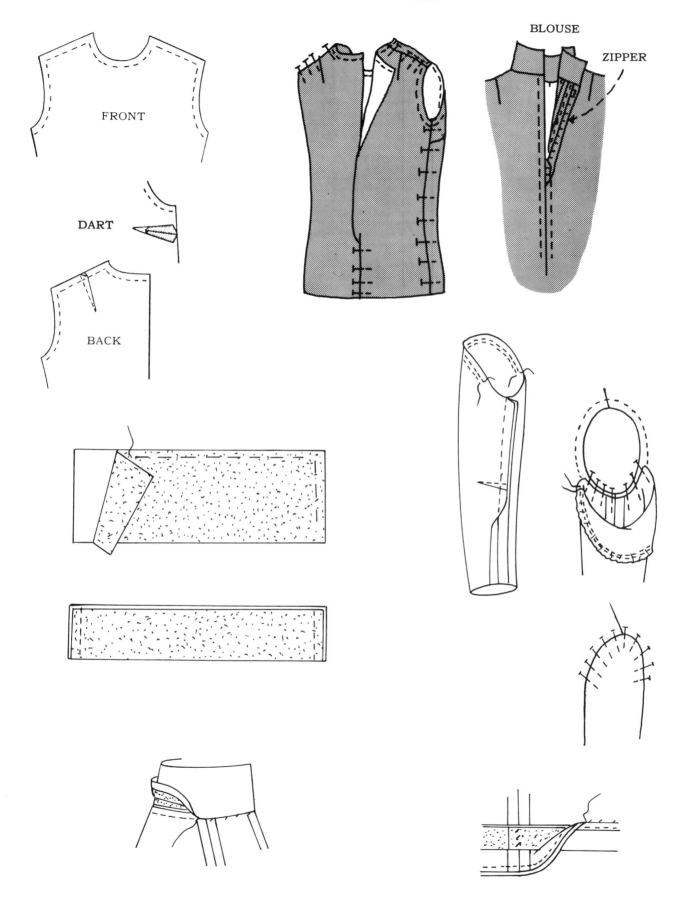

FRONT

DART

BACK

BLOUSE

ZIPPER

XIII

The Prize Package: Tailoring a Coat or Suit

FINE tailoring makes sewing an adventure—an interesting and vastly rewarding experience. Remember, devoted patience is a requisite to fulfill your objective of creating a couturier garment.

Begin with a simple coat or suit with few pieces to the pattern, using a fabric that tailors and presses easily. On your first tailored garments, concentrate on learning to *tailor*—not on mastering a difficult but stylish fabric. With a coat or suit it definitely pays to construct and fit a muslin pattern first. Then, bringing to bear all the couture techniques you've learned thus far, you're ready to produce a truly well-made wardrobe winner.

STEP-BY-STEP TO A COUTURE COAT OR SUIT

SELECTING THE FABRIC: For your first trip I suggest a fabric with a spongy wool texture since this type molds more easily when pressing. Worsteds, hard-textured wools and firmly woven fabrics are more difficult to work with. It's wise to experiment on this type of fabric by cutting a small piece, stitching a curved seam and steam pressing to indicate how the fabric will react.

Once you get the feel of a fabric you'll know better how to handle it. In ironing a hard-textured fabric, whether for a coat, suit or dress, you may achieve better results in pressing if you insert a thin cardboard between seam and garment, so that the imprint of the seam is not transferred to the right side of the fabric.

CUTTING THE UNDERLINING: Be sure your underlining is the right weight for the outer fabric (refer

to chart at end of Chapter 7 in making your selection). If your fabric is lightweight it may have to be built up with a heavier underlining; if thick or heavy it will require only a thin underlining. If the fabric is not dense, a heavier underlining in the same color as outer fabric will prevent the interfacing from showing through.

The underlining is cut exactly like the pattern of your coat or suit. Grain lines must be observed carefully for the underlining as well as the outer fabric. Transfer all construction markings to the underlining as described in Chapter 8.

CUTTING FACINGS: If your coat or suit has a lapel collar which is shaped, the facing of the garment will have to be seamed starting where the lapel begins. The rest of the facing can be cut in one with the garment. If possible, select a pattern with a facing included on the garment proper since this eliminates an edge seam which must be tailored very carefully.

WORKING WITH THE OUTER FABRIC: Place the different units of the underlining on the outer fabric, pin and measure grain lines to be sure they are perfect. Cut the garment and trace with a small basting stitch all construction marks through to the outer fabric so that all markings, including center front, armholes, collar mounting lines, buttonholes, etc., are clearly indicated on the right side of outer fabric.

INITIAL SEWING: (To hold the garment in place you can put a "stay" of lightweight Si Bonne or canvas across the shoulders and armholes in back). Stay stitch the neckline, armholes and lapels. Catch the underlining to the fold-line of garment with a small basting stitch or a blind stitch to secure underlining to outer fabric. Shoulders and neckline should be taped to prevent stretching. It is advisable to tape fold-line so that garment will not swing away.

DARTS: Next baste the darts. If you have a long curved dart, you may want to slash it within an inch from the point. Since tracing marks are transferred to the right side of fabric, pin the darts together on the right side for easier molding of the curve. Slip-baste the dart. I wouldn't recommend final stitching until entire garment is basted together and

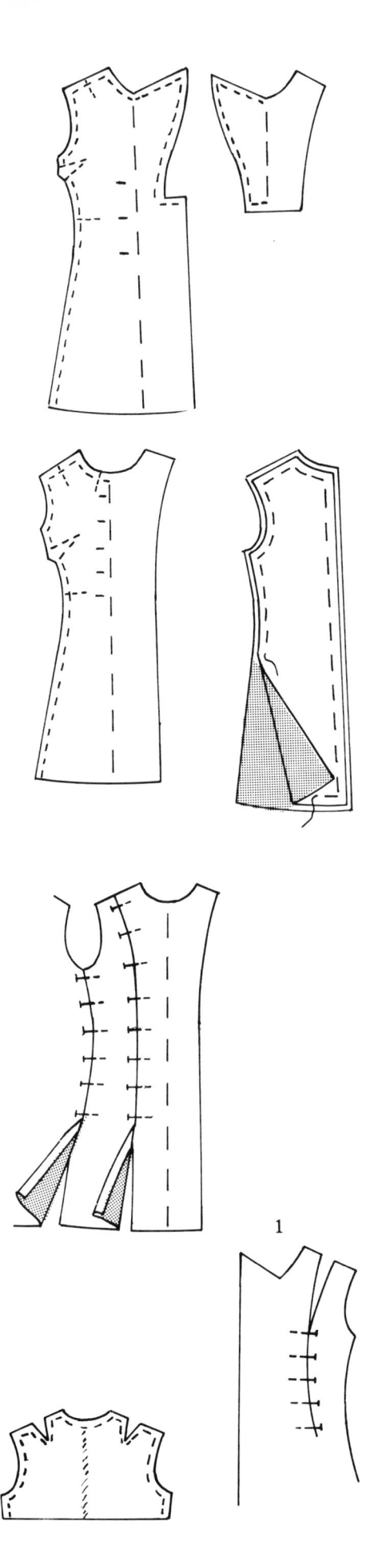

[85]

MAJOR CONSTRUCTION

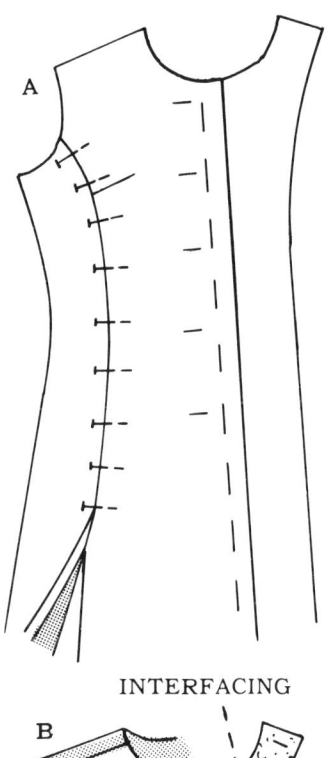

A

INTERFACING

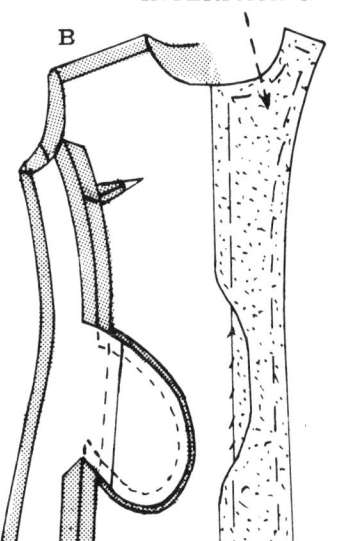

B

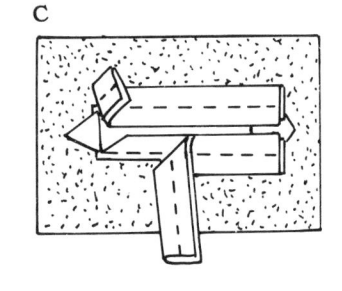

C

1. On the right side, pin or baste the front and back or side panels together and slip-baste. Repeat until all body seams are basted (2). Then try on. After trying on your coat or suit and making any alterations according to procedure previously described, you can begin the "important" sewing. It's helpful to separate the front from the back for easier handling. Then re-baste again after your buttonholes and facings are made. (A)

2. Remember, each unit must be pressed as it is stitched. Don't press hard. Always use a press cloth. When steaming the right side of a fabric, never place the iron directly on the cloth. Let the steam penetrate, and use a pounding block or the palm of your hand to flatten seams.

3. Now cut an interfacing of tailor's canvas or hair cloth (of weight dictated by your outer fabric). This interfacing should be cut exactly like the front of the garment and 1″ beyond fold line. It should extend into shoulders and front armholes and end just at the point of the bust (3, 4).

4. Next attach the interfacing, using padding stitches, heavier on the lapel and fold line and lighter on the rest of the interfacing. Catch only the underlining so that stitches will not show on outer fabric. Cut the canvas away on either side of the dart close to the seam line and catch to the underlining. Repeat at shoulder seams. (B)

5. If fabric is heavy make buttonholes before attaching the interfacing. I suggest trying a test buttonhole on a small scrap of fabric to verify the correct size.

6. After securing the interfacing, mark buttonhole slash lines on interfacing and cut the slash line a little longer so that interfacing will slip under the buttonhole strips without pulling the buttonhole (if fabric is heavy). Fasten with a small stitch by hand all around slash line. (C)

7. It's best to set interfacing into the garment by using a tailor's ham, with the right side of garment *up* since the curve of the cushion will mold the interfacing to the shape of the garment. Pin well and

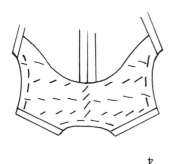

4

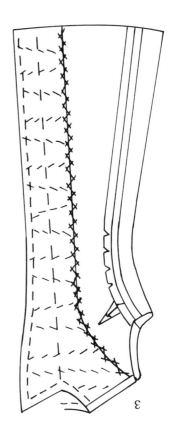

3

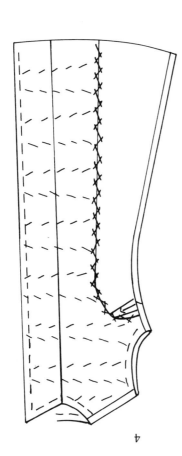

4

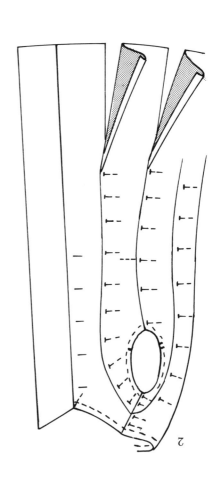

2

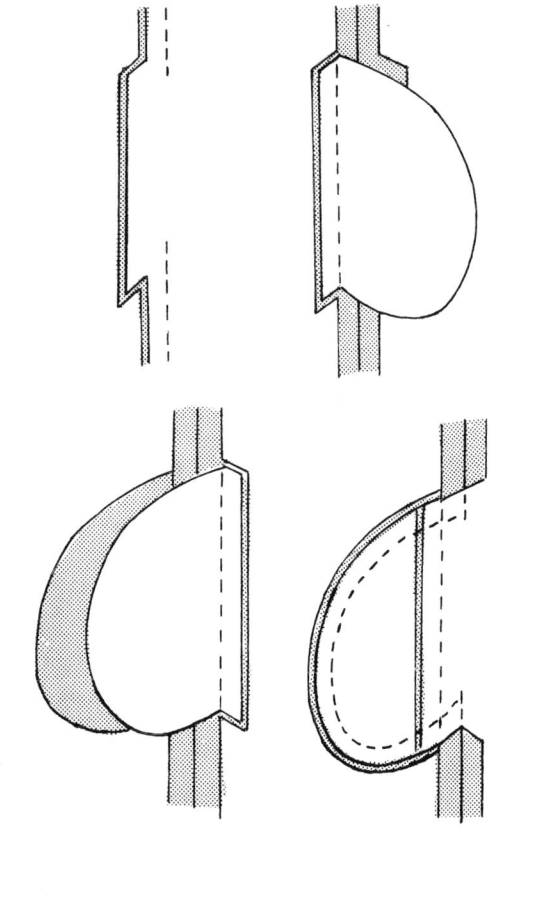

baste so that interfacing will not shift when removing it from the cushion. The interfacing gives the garment body and it will look professionally tailored.

8. If you are making pockets in the seam, do so while the garment is open.

9. After finishing buttonholes and pockets, place the front and back or side panel right side up and turn under one seam allowance and place over the seam allowance of the opposite unit, matching all construction markings, cross marks or notches. Place pins diagonally to seam and slip-baste so that stitch shows on the wrong side. Repeat for all other body seams, and try on again.

10. If alterations are necessary, make them; then stitch seams on the wrong side. Press seams *open*. After seams are pressed, sew shoulders the same way.

COAT OR SUIT COLLARS

For a coat or suit collar, follow this technique (full details in Chapter 11). The underlining has already been attached.

1. Seam back of collar; press open. Attach the interfacing. Don't lap interfacing at back seam; instead, cut it to meet this seam and connect with a catch stitch (5). Use a long padding stitch to attach interfacing to undercollar—closer padding stitches at neck and roll line and cross stitches all around the sewing line of the curved edge. Cut the corners of the canvas for a blunt edge and trim around the curved edge close to the stitching line. The padding stitches can be caught here and there to the outer fabric of the undercollar to give more firmness.

2. Baste the upper collar to the undercollar right sides together, leaving bottom edge open to attach to neckline. Turn collar to right side, baste around the outer edge, pulling out the seam and points as you do. Lightly steam; do not press.

3. Shape undercollar by placing on a tailor's ham, using steam *only* and your hand to acquire proper shape and roll. A thick cotton roll placed under roll line is very helpful.

4. Place upper collar over undercollar, shaping it on ham. Start pinning at neck; be sure to leave

5

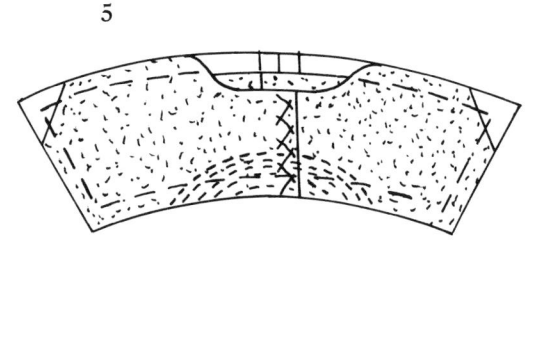

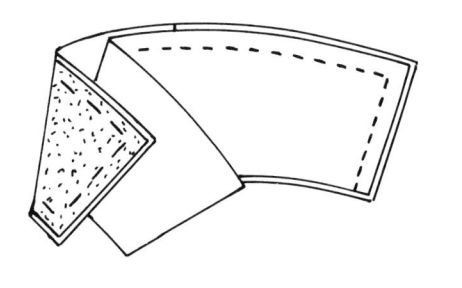

enough fabric for roll line so that collar lies flat. Pin toward outer edge and baste. Examine collar to check roll line.

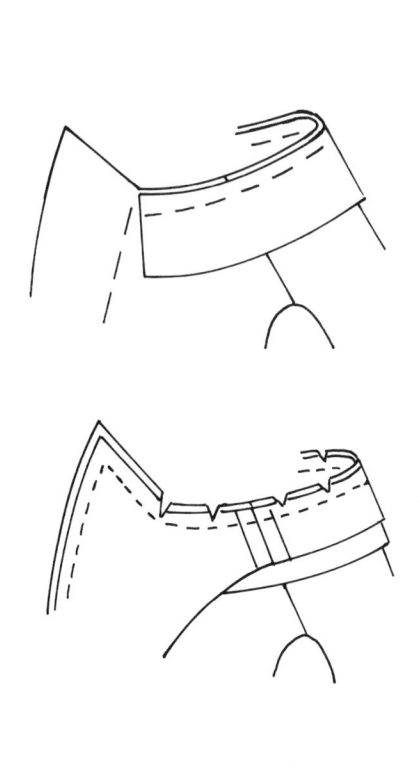

5. Mark new seam line on upper collar. Re-pin and re-baste, using new seam line of upper collar. Place collar, right sides together; baste and stitch outside ends and curved edge. Leave open section to be attached at neckline. Clip rounded edges; turn to right side.

6. Pull out rounded edges and corners of collar with needle or pin. Baste edge. Steam collar on tailor's ham, flattening the seam slightly with palm of your hand or pounding block. Re-shape the roll line; then, remove basting.

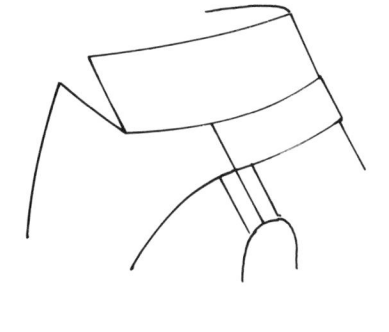

7. Pin and baste undercollar right sides together to neckline of garment, starting at center back to finish line at front of neck or lapel. Stitch; press seam *open*.

8. Baste overcollar down, starting at center back, and attach to facings in front. Stitch only area where collar and facings join. Press this seam open. The back of overcollar should face *down* so that lining may be sewn to it.

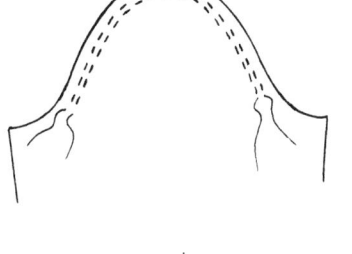

9. Secure front and back collar with a blind stitch, sewing through the stitching line where facing and collar join.

SLEEVES FOR COATS AND SUITS

Follow this procedure for sleeves. A tailored sleeve with a lap closing is usually cut with an undersleeve which makes a two-piece sleeve. The back seam forms the lap which is in line with the small finger of your hand.

1. Underline the sleeve and baste the seams. Ease in cap of sleeve. Try on to check the width before stitching. If everything is right, stitch the seams, the back seam only to vent opening. Clip the back seam, underlap $5/8''$ above opening point. Press seams open and the vent forward.

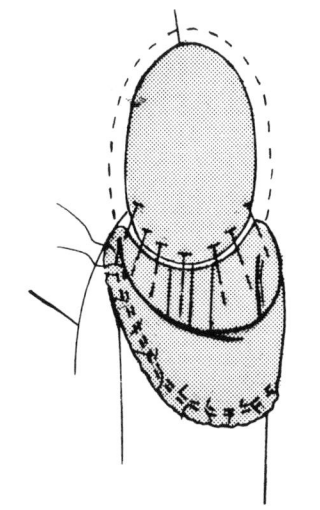

2. Cut a bias facing $1\frac{1}{2}''$ wider than the hem and $1''$ wider than the vent seam allowance. For the hem allow an extra inch beyond the fold line. The vent interfacing is cut only to the fold line. This interfacing will conceal the marks from pressing and maintain the shape of the sleeve. Attach the interfacing

[89]

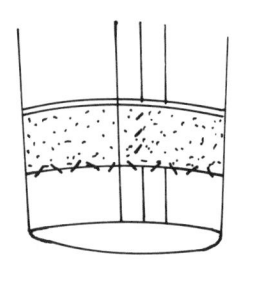

6   LINING

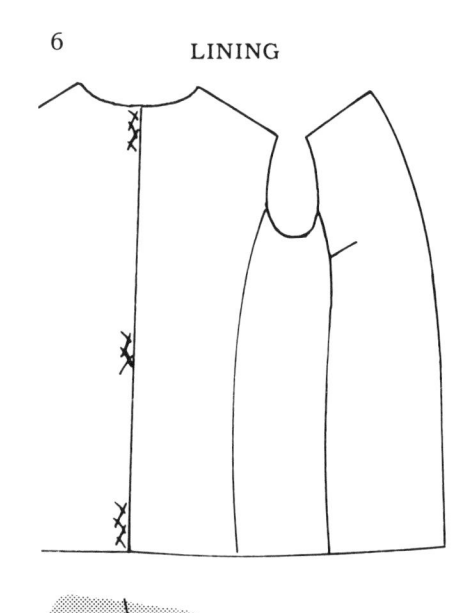

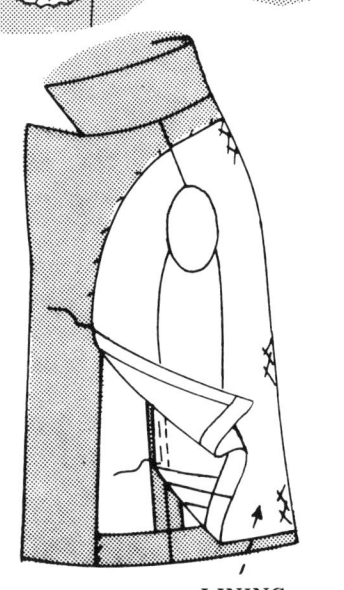

LINING

to underlining with catch stitch. Turn the underlap back close to seam binding and the upper lap on seam allowance.

3. If the interfacing and wool are heavy, make the buttonholes first, and then attach the interfacing. Slash it to slip under buttonholes without pulling and attach by hand. If the fabric and interfacing are lightweight you can make the buttonholes right through the interfacing.

4. For a regular hem on a sleeve, cut the interfacing 1½″ wide and 1″ beyond the fold line and attach with a catch stitch. Run a long basting stitch in the fold line to secure the interfacing.

5. A small shoulder pad does wonders to support the shape of the shoulders. This should be attached to garment before lining is put in. Pin to shoulders and try on for proper adjustment. Then attach to interfacing and shoulder seams.

HOW TO LINE A COAT OR SUIT

1. Cut lining and stay-stitch shoulders, neckline and armhole. Stitch the darts, side seams and shoulders. Press (6).

2. Baste center back fold and press lightly. Place garment and lining wrong sides together and pin matching side seams and shoulders. Turn back the front of the lining and sew seam allowance of the lining to seam allowance of garment with a long running stitch.

3. Turn in lap, pin and baste the lining to front facings, hem and neckline, catching it all around armhole. Fasten center back fold (with cross stitches on right side) at neck, waist and hem.

4. Run a double sewing line around cap of sleeve, leaving threads to pull at both ends. Stitch seam on sleeve lining and press. Slide lining over the sleeve, wrong sides together, and attach to underarm seam. Pin the cap, matching cross marks or notches and adjust the ease to fit the armhole. Tack the lining to seam and shoulder to secure it. Finish entire lining with a slip stitch.

5. Baste sleeve lining about 3″ up from edge of sleeve. Allow ½″ of ease so that the sleeve won't pull up. Turn under seam allowance and slip-stitch.

[90]

How to Give Fashions the Longest Life Ever

XIV

As fickle as the weather is, so too are the dictates of fashion. It would seem that no sooner have you lopped off every possible inch from your wardrobe than skirt lengths drop—and there you are with knees unfashionably showing, and your closet unfashionably empty. Or perhaps you've succumbed to a sleeveless rage—and, suddenly, pretty sleeves are back in the picture. There's no need to go into details. It's happened to all of us and the frightening end result is that familiar cry "I haven't a thing to wear!"

Well, obviously you can't discard your entire wardrobe to keep up with fashion's whims. And when you've worked hard building a collection of fine clothes, who would want to discard them anyway? At the same time, I disagree with that old saw "If you keep an outfit long enough, fashion will eventually come around to the same look." I say that unworn clothes clutter up closets. Why wait for them to come back in style. With imagination and your sewing machine you can keep your wardrobe *au courant* and newly interesting. Try some of my favorite ways to insure eternal life for well-made fashions.

Couture Tips

▪ If your clothes are too short and there isn't enough hem to let down, add a border of contrast fabric and color. The best way to do this is with a simulated leather or vinyl fabric in a contrasting color. Or try for a varied texture in contrasting hue. Tie the look together by repeating the added fabric or leather somewhere else on the dress—a belt, band at neck

and sleeve, etc. The end result will look as if the dress had been originally designed with these touches.

- Give a sleeveless dress a new look by molding it closer to the body via belting and wearing it with a matte jersey or Banlon sweater with a turtleneck. This turns your dress into a guimpe—especially effective if you match the belt to the sweater or jersey.

- Make a loose shift more fashionable-looking by taking in the side seams and putting in a dart from the bust to the hips. If the dress allows, take the dart from the shoulder to hip over the bust—an easy seam to fit.

- Add a ruffle at the hem to lengthen or change the total look of a dress. Consider crepe or wool with a taffeta ruffle—crepe with a lace ruffle—velvet with taffeta, organza or lace ruffle—print crepe with solid organza in a color tied to the print—black and white print with black organza ruffles.

- Dramatize an old stand-by with the addition of braided trim at the neck, sleeve and hem. In many cases, braid can also be used down the front of a dress—from neckline to hem and as belting as well. For cocktail and evening wear, the elegant braid choice might be a metallic variety in gold or silver.

- A short-sleeve dress that does nothing can be translated into a guimpe that means something! Simply cut out the sleeves, cut down the neck and wear your new jumper with a shirt or sweater blouse.

- Embellish a dress that's all too basic with a perky fresh white collar and cuffs in linen. Or use taffeta, or velvet in a compatible color. Add to the look with a pussy-cat bow of taffetta or organza in a contrasting color.

- Play the accessories game—tie a handkerchief scarf around the neck, blend the color to the dress, add a belt, and even you won't recognize last season's old-faithful.

- If it's too dated, then cut the top off and turn your aged dress into an update skirt to be worn with a shirt.

- Dramatize evening and cocktail fashions by adding rayon fringe, spaghetti fringe, feathers and, literally, baubles, bangles and beads.

My Catalog
of Basic
Designer
Fashions

CHART OF BODY MEASUREMENTS

FOR PATTERNS BY ROXANE IN THIS BOOK

SIZE	8	10	12	14	16	18	20
BUST	34½	35¾	37	39	40½	42	42¾
WAIST	24½	25½	27	28	29¾	31	32½
HIPS	35	36¼	37½	38¾	40½	42	43½

The sizes used in patterns in the back of this book are different from commercial patterns and approximately equivalent to the sizes of ready-to-wear clothes. Manufacturers, whether boutique or couture, employ a standard measurement chart supplied by the industry. Measurements may vary slightly, depending on the manufacturer; some like to have their clothes fit very closely to the figure and others allow for ease. But basically they do not change to any great degree. If you wear a size 10 in ready-to-wear, it would be safe to select a size 10 pattern.

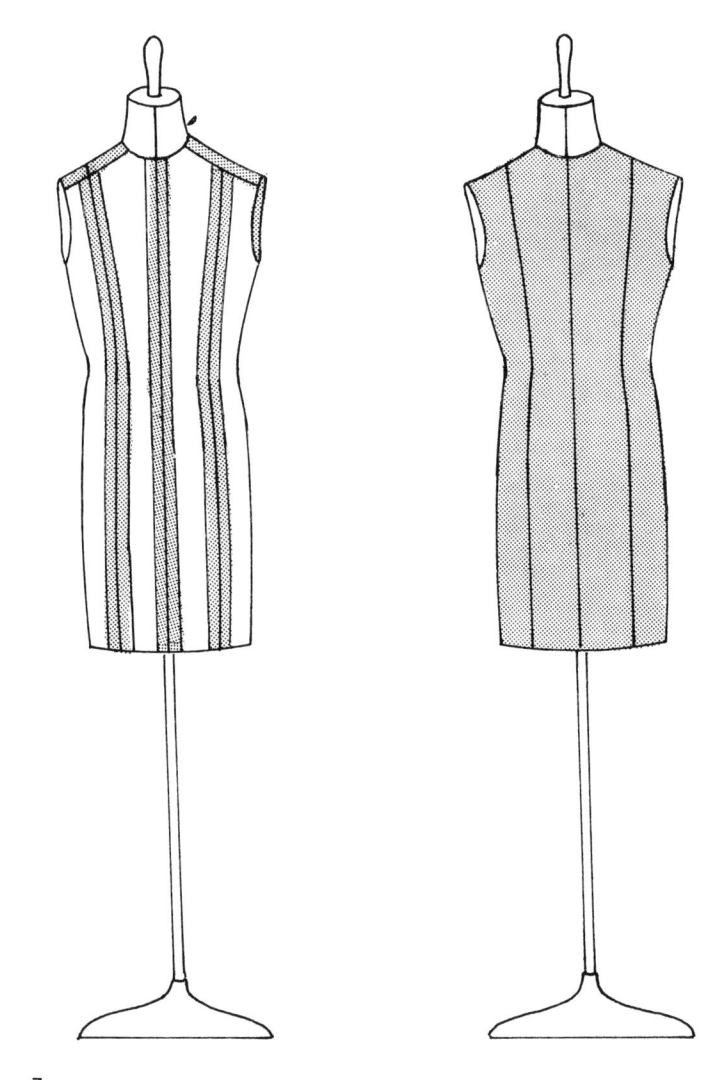

TO ORDER PATTERNS

Custom couturier patterns for all styles shown in this book can be obtained from Roxane.

Prices for patterns, including postage, are:

SKIRTS	$2.50
DRESSES	$4.00
PANTS SUITS	$4.50
COATS	$4.50

Send money order or check to:

ROXANE
923 Fifth Ave.
New York City, N.Y. 10021

New York State residents must add appropriate sales tax.

1   *Flared skirt with six gores*

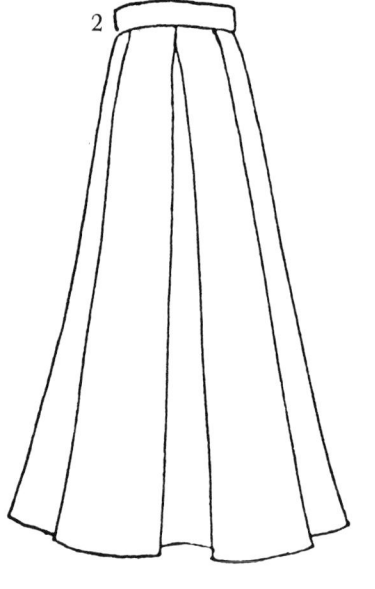

2   *Slightly A-line with two front,
graduated box pleats*

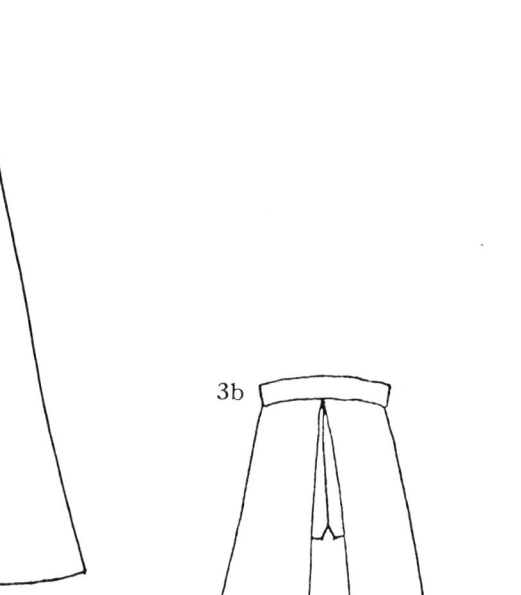

3   *Front invert pleat with wide
top-stitching on both sides*

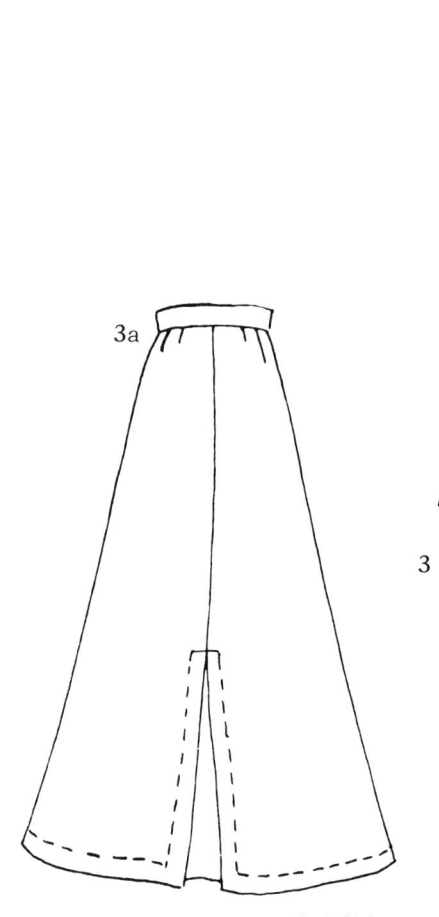

3a   *A-line skirt with low slit. Wide
top-stitching around hem and slit.*

3b   *Slightly A-line skirt slit to waist can
be worn over jump suit or shorts.*

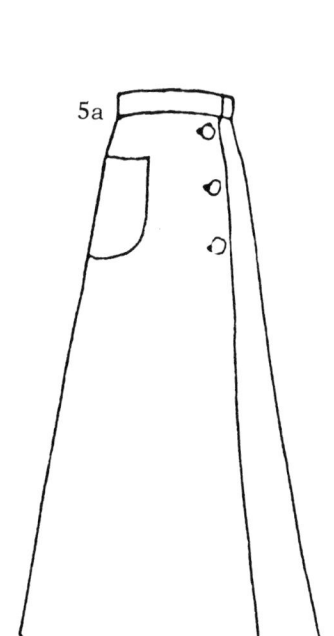

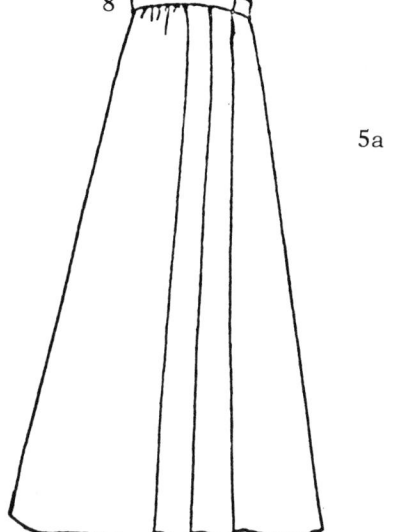

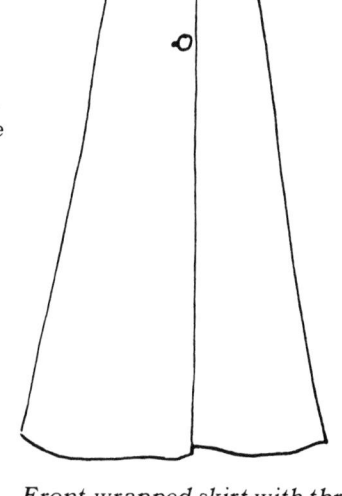

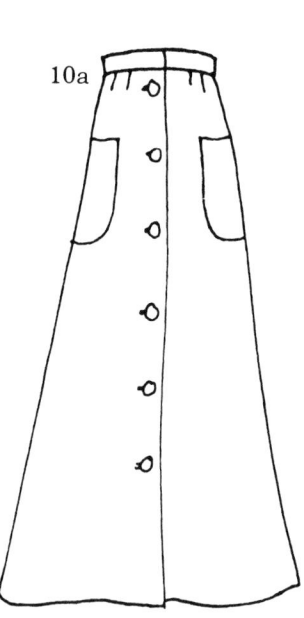

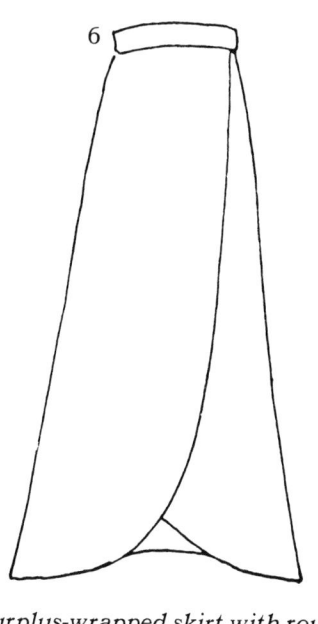

5   Hip-wrapped skirt buttoned to hem
     and top-stitched.

6   Surplus-wrapped skirt with rounded
     hem.

5a   Side-wrapped skirt with three buttons
     and patch pocket.

8   Side-wrapped skirt with two deep side
     pleats.

10a Front-buttoned skirt with two patch
     pockets.

10   Front-wrapped skirt with three
     buttons. Pockets can be added.

DRESSES

310 *Street dress, can be belted if preferred.*

Wool—braid or velvet banding
Heavy crepe—taffeta or satin banding
Wool jersey—velvet or self banding
Woven cotton print—self banding
Solid color cotton

214 *Shirtwaist dress, open front wrap and two patch pockets (not cut-through waistline).*

Wool solid or print
Wool jersey
Polyester knit or heavy matte jersey
Heavy crepe
Cotton
Velvet or brocade for cocktail wear

215 Coat dress or one-piece shirtwaist
      dress with open lap front, four
      flap pockets.
   Wool
   Wool jersey
   Woven cotton
   Polyester knit
   Satin or brocade for cocktail

216 Double-breasted coat dress.
   Wool
   Wool jersey or polyester knit
   Heavy woven cotton

306 Guimpe dress to be worn with a
      shirt or sweater blouse.
   Wool
   Wool jersey or polyester knit

[99]

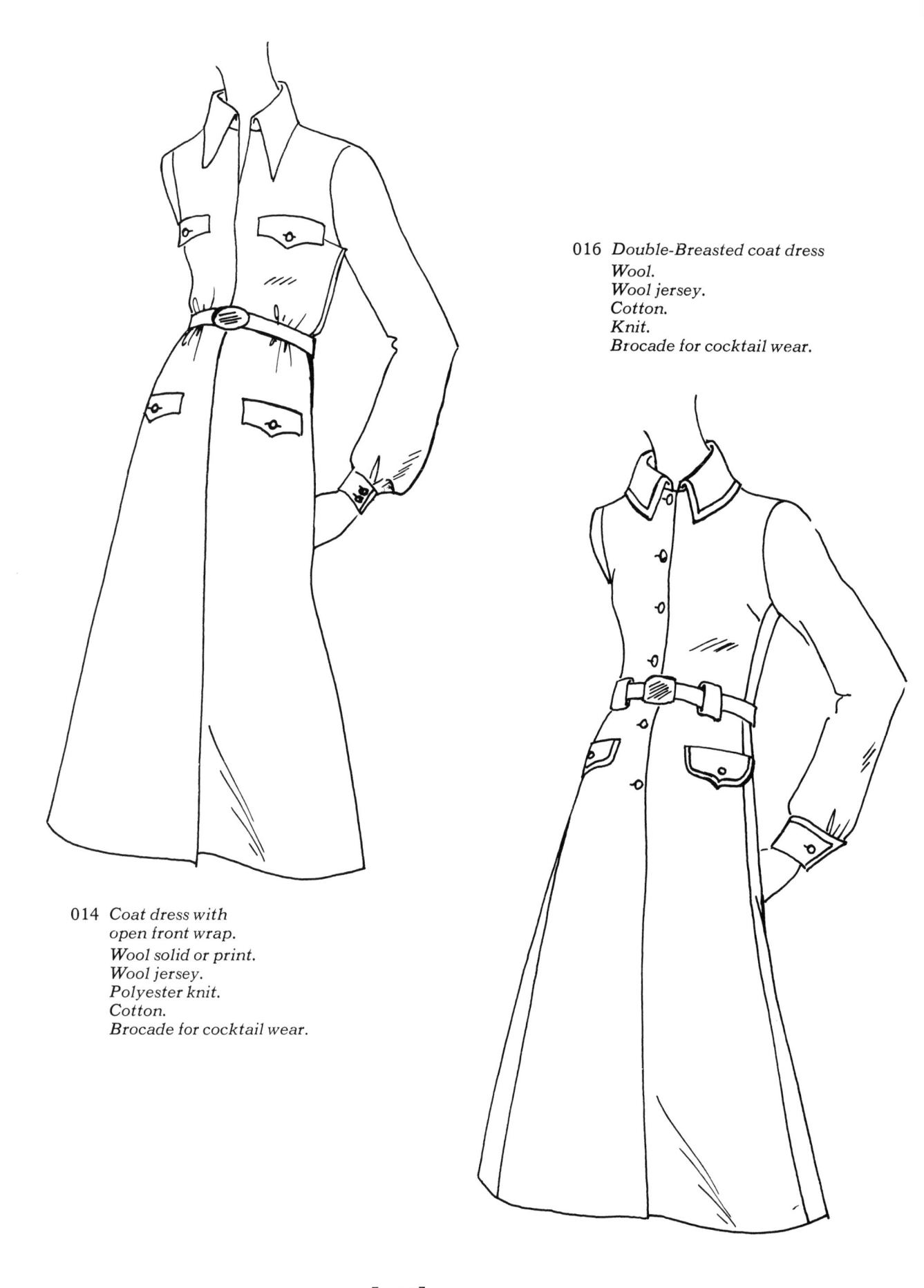

016 Double-Breasted coat dress
     Wool.
     Wool jersey.
     Cotton.
     Knit.
     Brocade for cocktail wear.

014 Coat dress with
     open front wrap.
     Wool solid or print.
     Wool jersey.
     Polyester knit.
     Cotton.
     Brocade for cocktail wear.

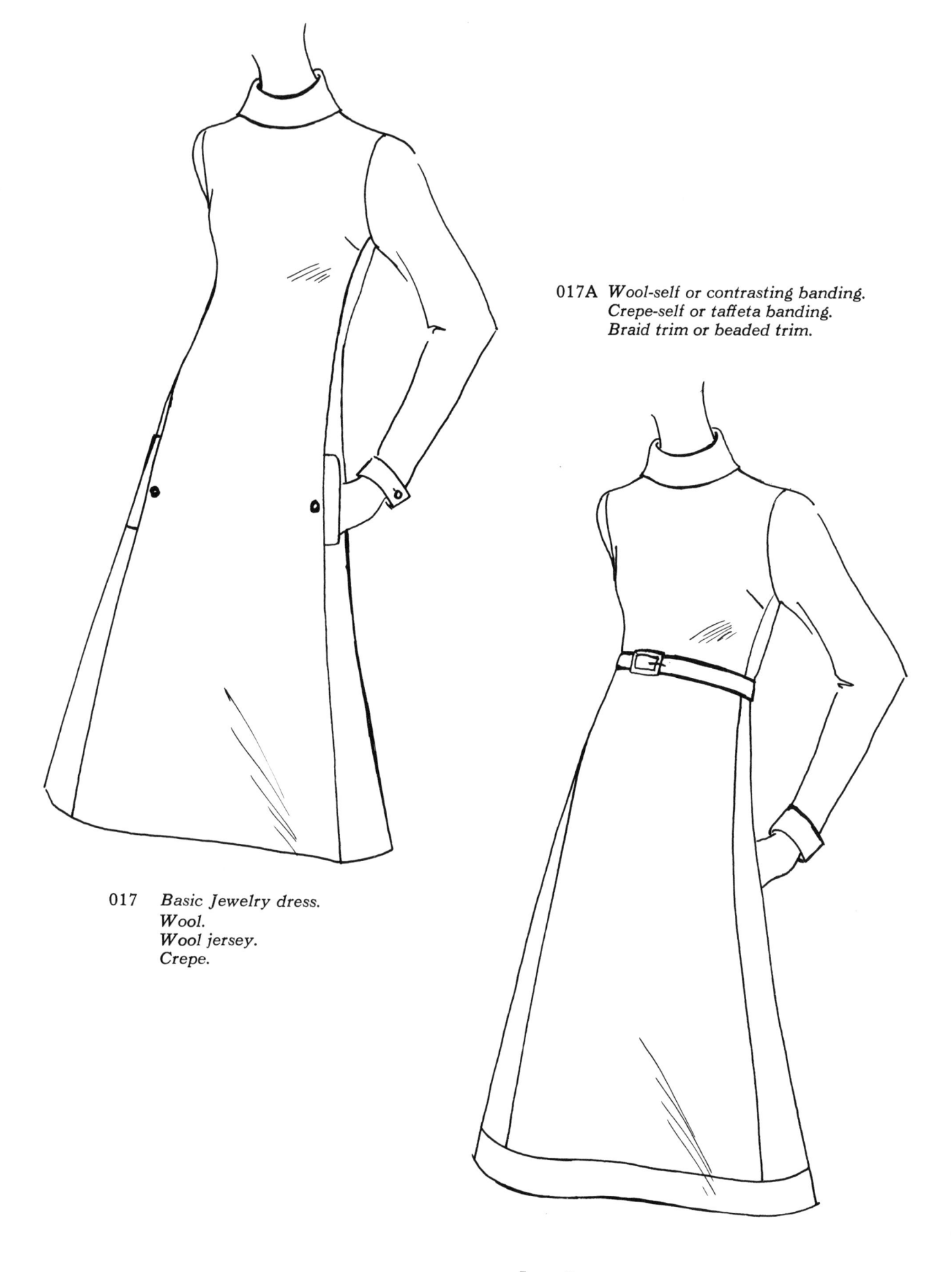

017A *Wool-self or contrasting banding.*
Crepe-self or taffeta banding.
Braid trim or beaded trim.

017 *Basic Jewelry dress.*
Wool.
Wool jersey.
Crepe.

PANTS SUITS

315

315 *Cardigan-jacket pants suit, solid or
      contrasting jacket.*
      Wool or wool jersey
      Polyester knit

316

316 *Shirt-top pants suit, slit on sides.*
      Wool jersey
      Matte jersey
      Polyester knit

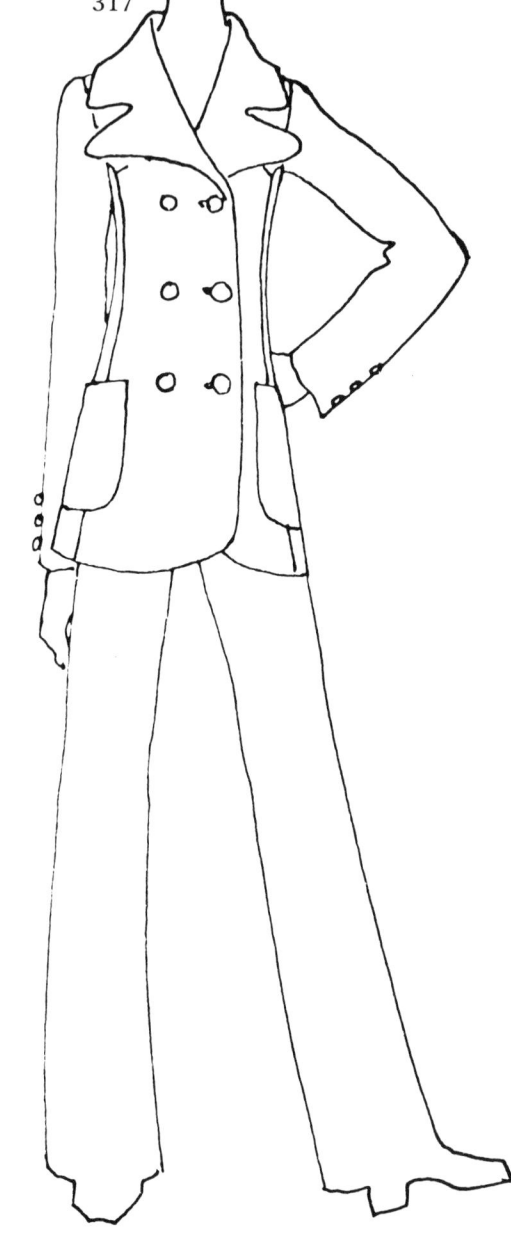

317 *Blazer-jacket, double-breasted
     pants suit.*
     Wool or wool jersey

318 *Trench-coat jacket, self tie belt.*
     Wool
     Heavy wool jersey or knit

319 *Sleeveless sweater-top pants suit to be worn with shirts or sweater blouse.*

Wool or wool jersey
Knit fabric
Simulated leather (for the top only)

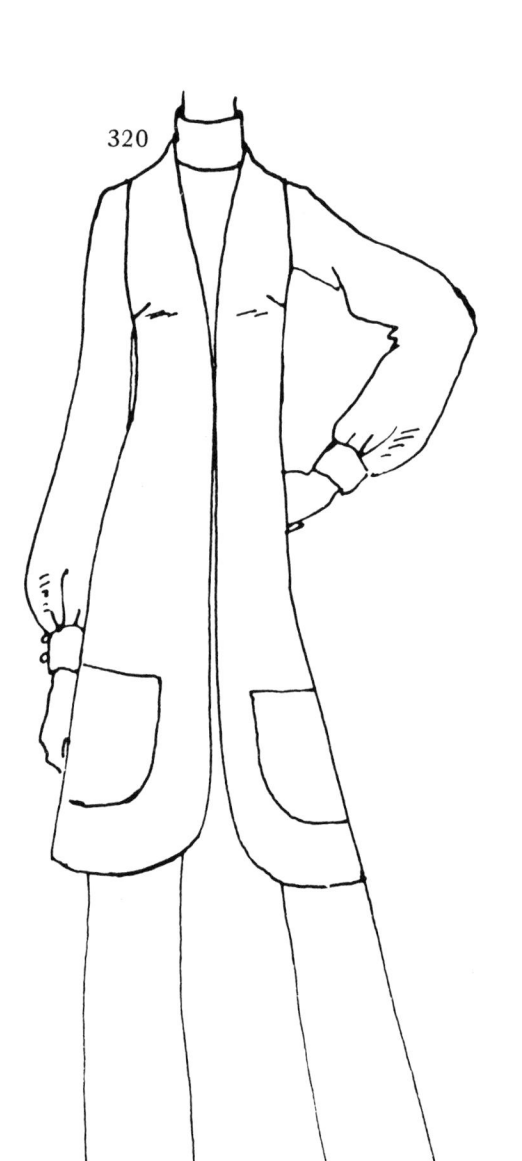

320 *Sleeveless-cardigan coat to knee. Solid or contrast color combinations.*
Wool or wool jersey

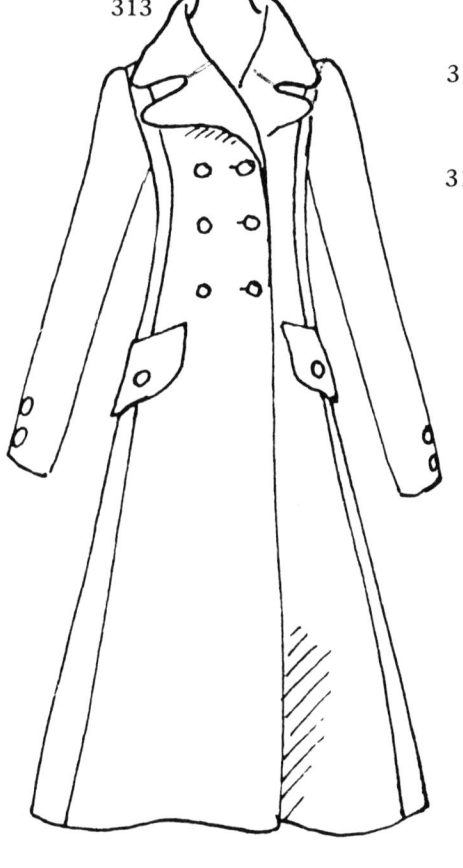

311

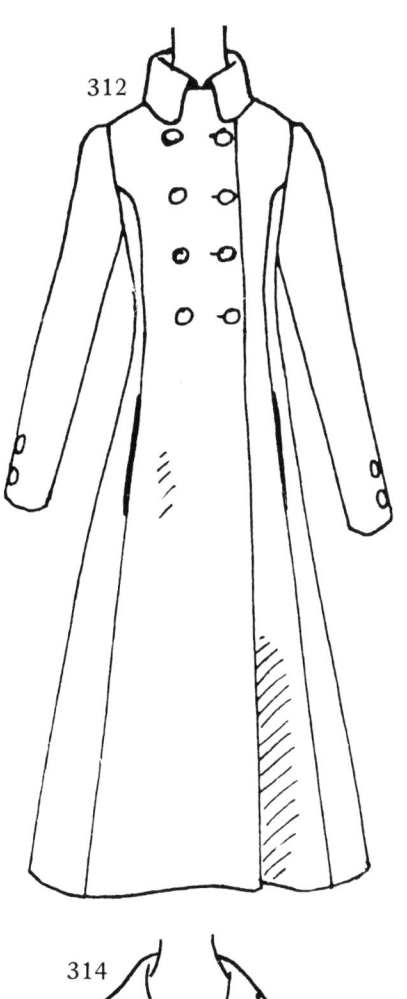

312

311 *Belted coat with tailored sleeve.*
   Wool or heavy wool jersey
   Simulated leather
   Heavy-woven cotton
   Silk solid or print if backed with
   *   tailor's canvas*
   Brocade

312 *Double-breasted A-line, can be*
   *   worn belted.*
   Wool or wool jersey
   Heavy woven cotton
   Brocade

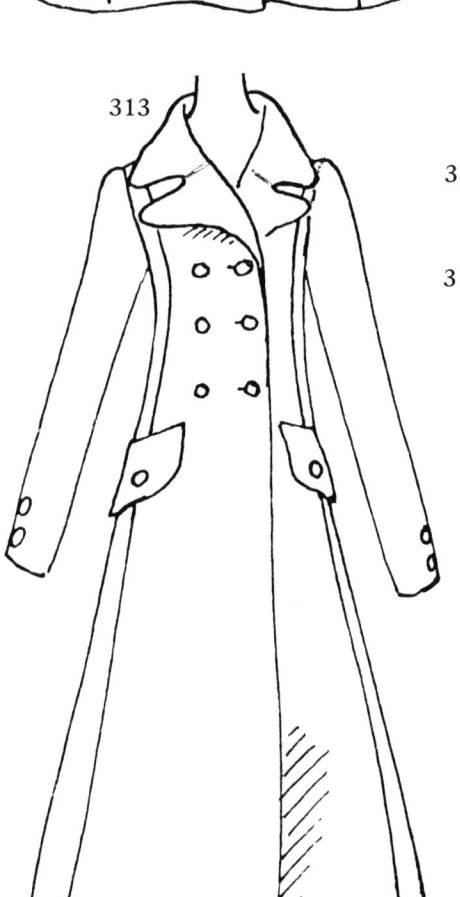

313

314

313 *Double-breasted reefer.*
   Wool
   Heavy wool jersey or knit

314 *Trench coat, self tie belt.*
   Wool
   Heavy wool jersey or knit

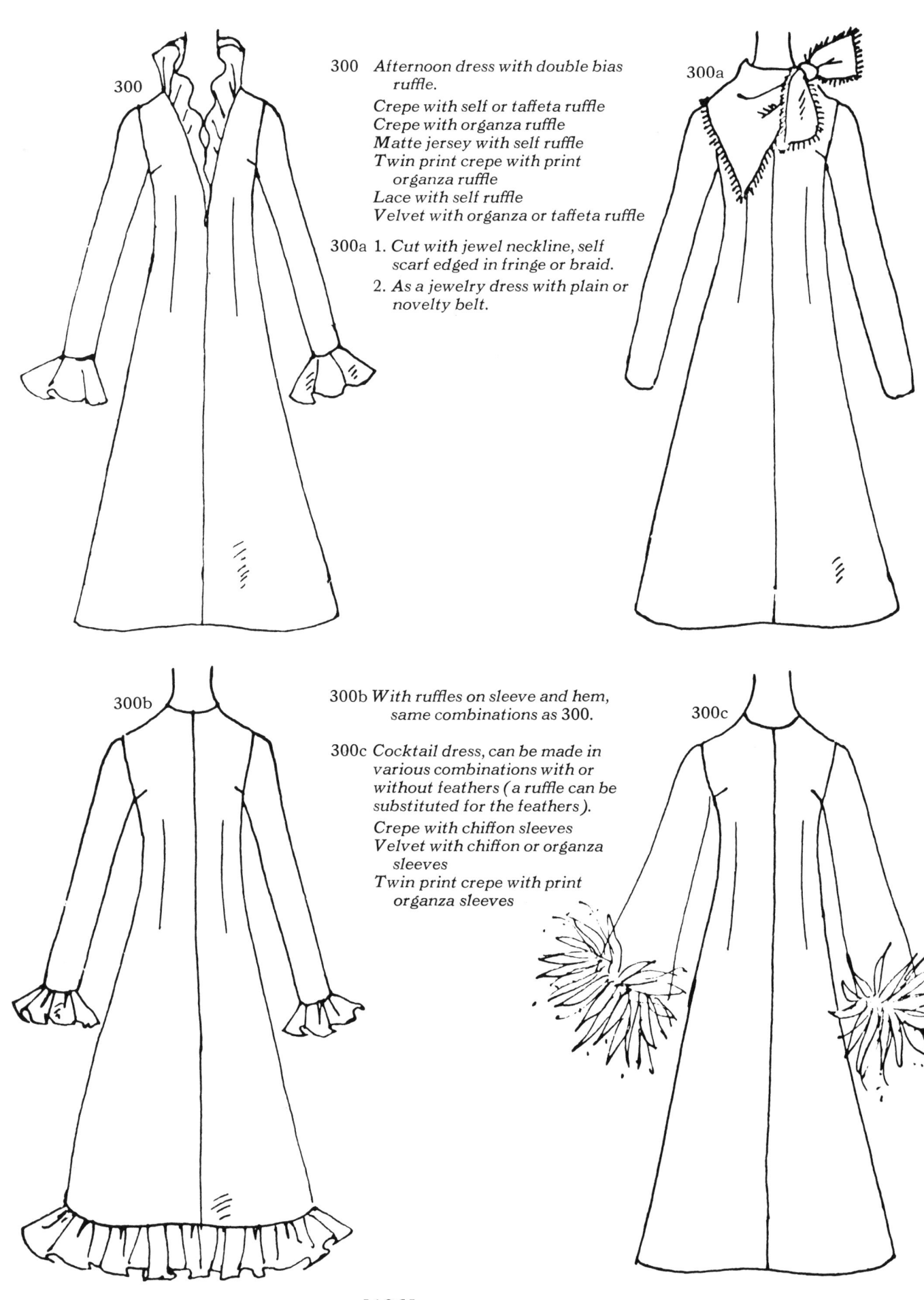

300 *Afternoon dress with double bias ruffle.*

Crepe with self or taffeta ruffle
Crepe with organza ruffle
Matte jersey with self ruffle
Twin print crepe with print organza ruffle
Lace with self ruffle
Velvet with organza or taffeta ruffle

300a 1. *Cut with jewel neckline, self scarf edged in fringe or braid.*

2. *As a jewelry dress with plain or novelty belt.*

300b *With ruffles on sleeve and hem, same combinations as 300.*

300c *Cocktail dress, can be made in various combinations with or without feathers (a ruffle can be substituted for the feathers).*

Crepe with chiffon sleeves
Velvet with chiffon or organza sleeves
Twin print crepe with print organza sleeves

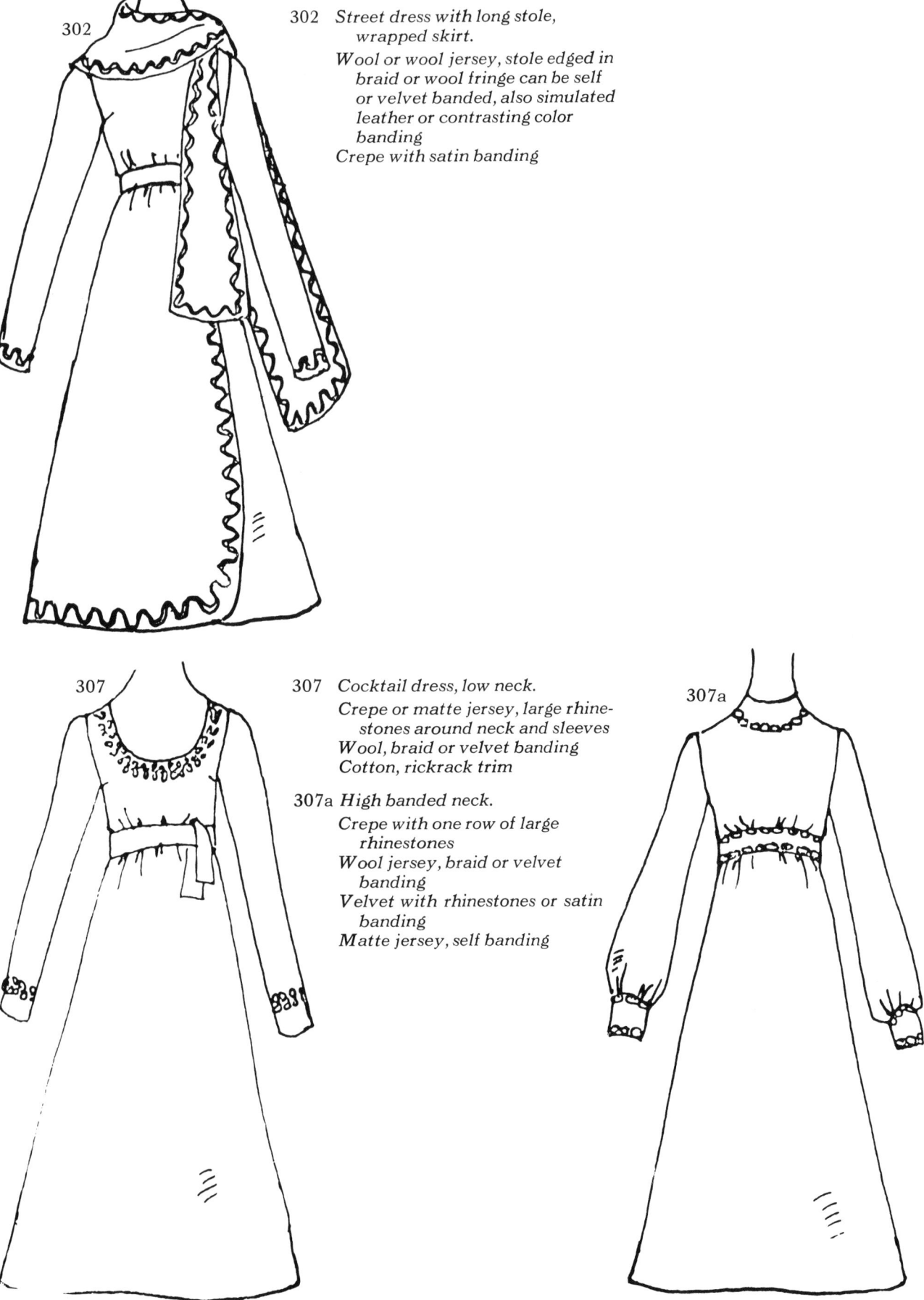

302 Street dress with long stole,
     wrapped skirt.
     *Wool or wool jersey, stole edged in
     braid or wool fringe can be self
     or velvet banded, also simulated
     leather or contrasting color
     banding*
     Crepe with satin banding

307 Cocktail dress, low neck.
     *Crepe or matte jersey, large rhine-
     stones around neck and sleeves*
     Wool, braid or velvet banding
     Cotton, rickrack trim

307a High banded neck.
     *Crepe with one row of large
     rhinestones*
     *Wool jersey, braid or velvet
     banding*
     *Velvet with rhinestones or satin
     banding*
     Matte jersey, self banding

418

418 Evening shirtwaist dress, deep-
fold-front skirt.
Crepe solid or contrasting top
Chiffon brocade
Twin print crepe skirt, chiffon or
organza top
Heavy brocade
Matte jersey
Velvet solid or combined with
chiffon or organza

419

419 Evening dress, low neck, side-wrap
skirt.
Crepe with wide shirred-lace ruffle
Crepe with wide shirred-taffeta
ruffle
Velvet with organza ruffle
Twin print crepe dress, print
organza ruffle
Organza, self ruffle

420

420 Evening dress, low V-neckline.
Ruffle can be shirred or circular.
Crepe with self or lace ruffle
Velvet with organza or taffeta
Twin print crepe dress chiffon or
organza print ruffle
Organza self ruffle
Matte jersey self ruffle

[108]

421

421 *Sophisticated simple evening dress with or without trim. Excellent as a jewelry dress. Can be belted.*

Crepe
Matte jersey
Wool crepe

422

422 *Fitted princess-line evening dress, low or high neck, jeweled midriff belt. Can also be worn with a patent belt and gold buckle and gold jewelry.*

Crepe
Matte jersey
Wool crepe

CONSTRUCTION SKETCHES

SLEEVES
EASE STITCH

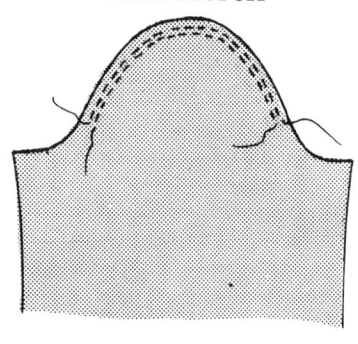

SLEEVE WITH CASING

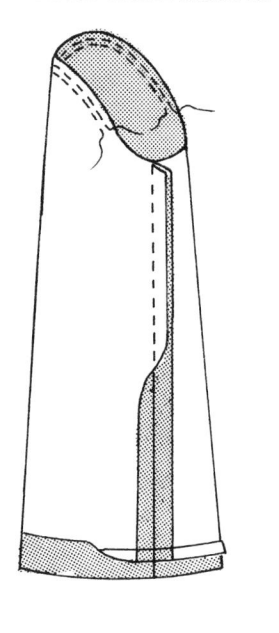

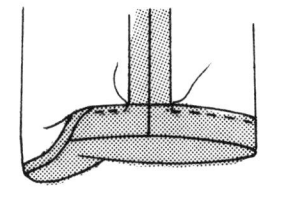

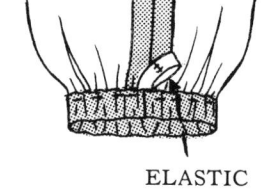

ELASTIC

SHIRT-SLEEVE

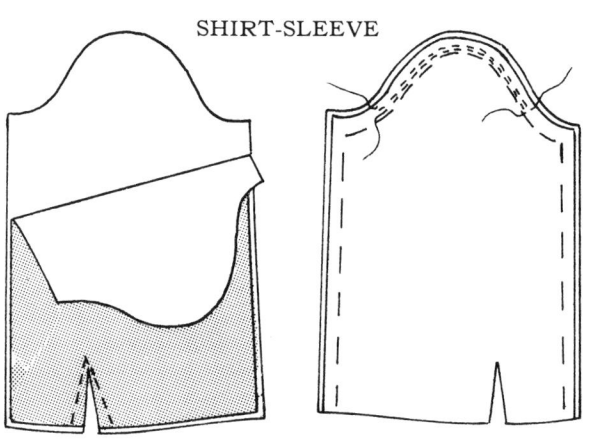

BAND CUFF

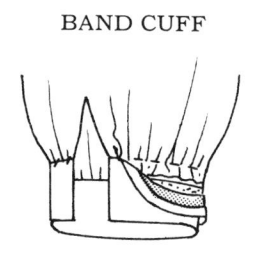

SETTING IN SLEEVES RIGHT SIDES TOGETHER

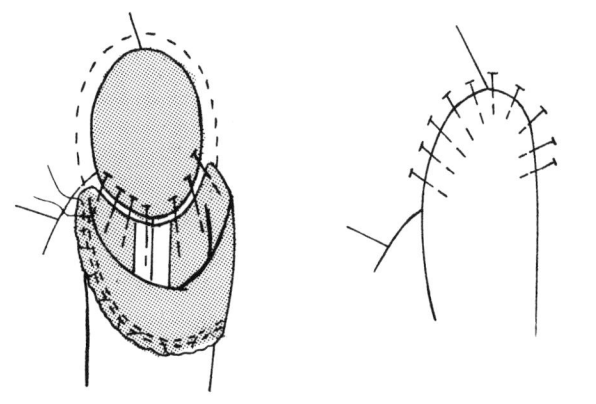

ON WRONG SIDE TOGETHER

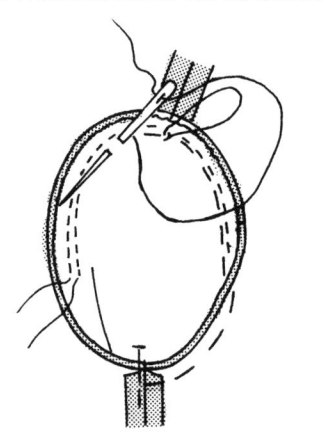

[110]

STRAIGHT SLEEVE

ONE PIECE
TAILORED SLEEVE

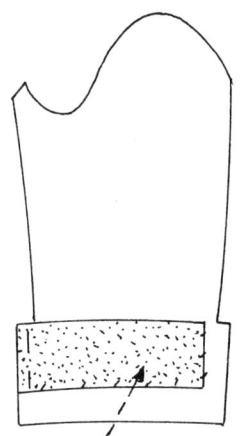

INTERFACING

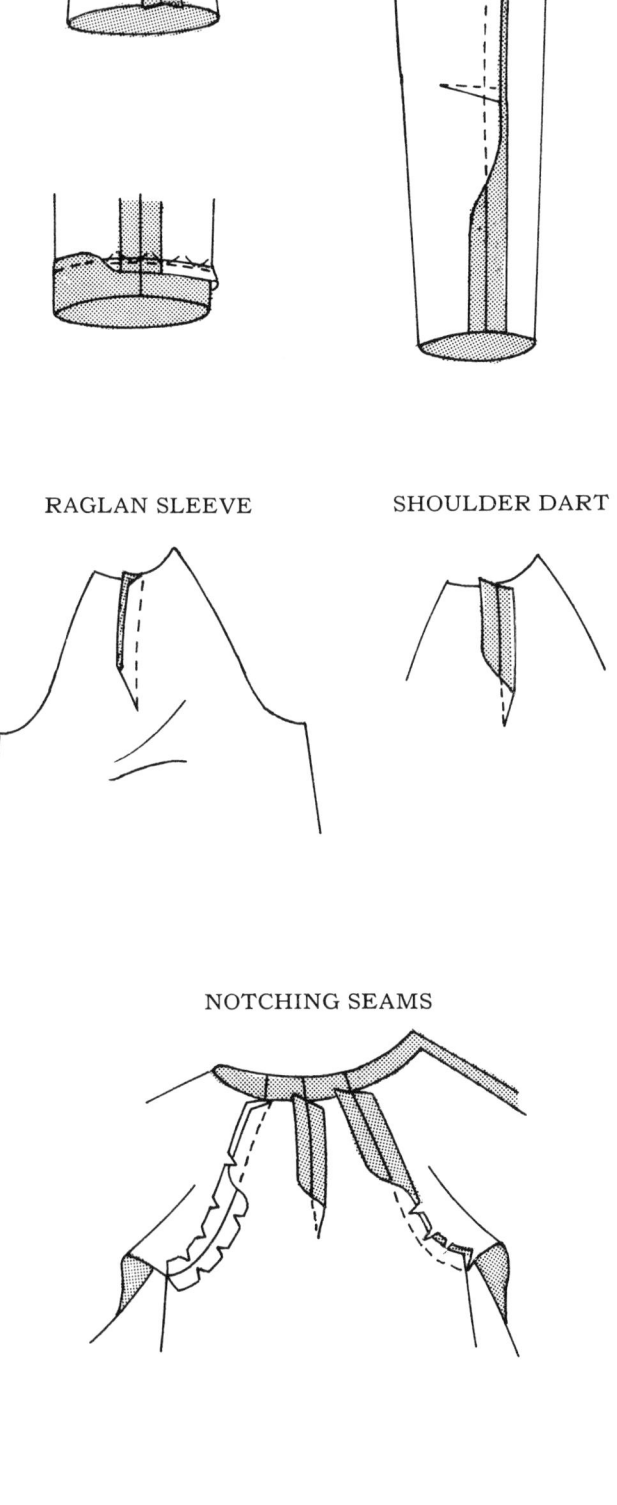

RAGLAN SLEEVE

SHOULDER DART

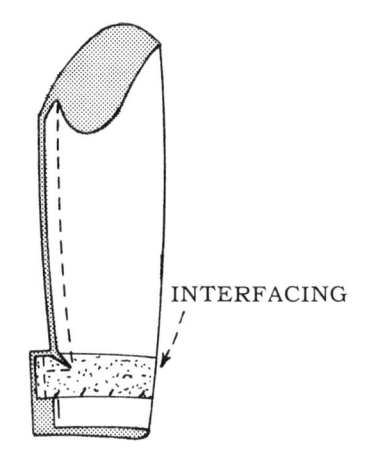

INTERFACING

NOTCHING SEAMS

INTERFACING

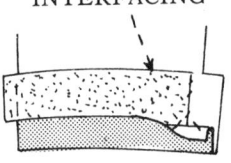

SLEEVE HEM

INTERFACING

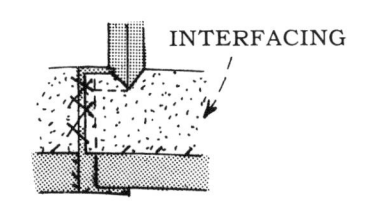

[111]

CUFF BAND

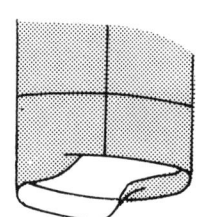

TAILORED SLEEVE

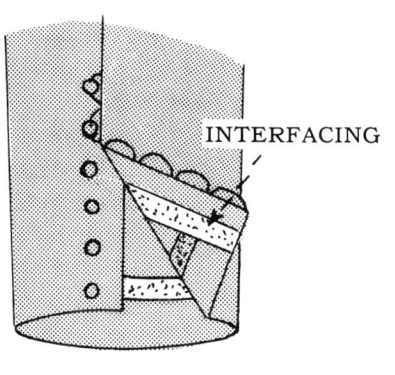

INTERFACING

INTERFACING

MOUNT BAND

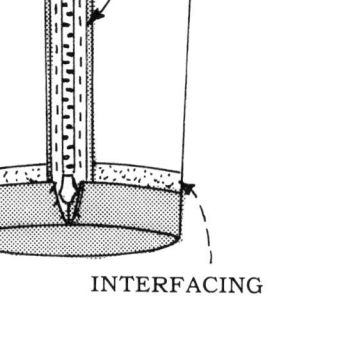

TURN UNDER
EDGE OF SLEEVE

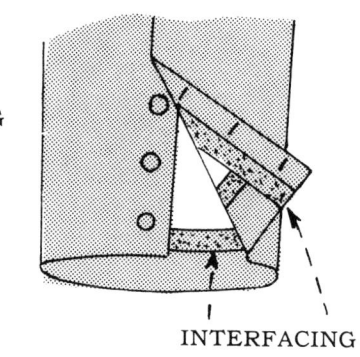

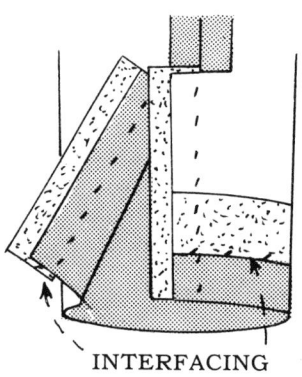

INTERFACING

ZIPPER

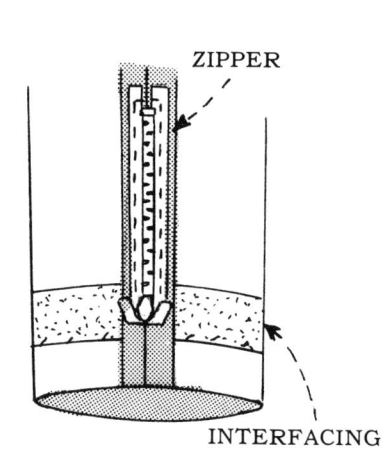

INTERFACING

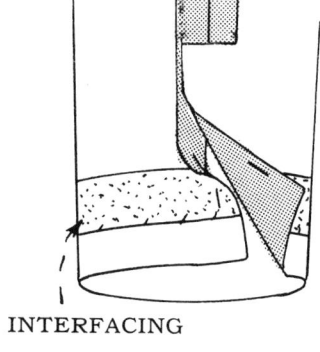

INTERFACING

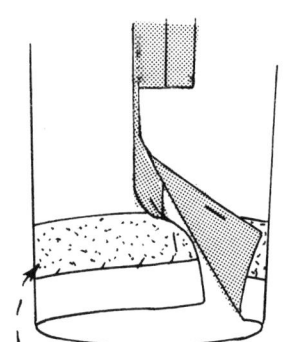

INTERFACING

ZIPPER

INTERFACING

[112]

BOUND BUTTONHOLE

BUTTONHOLE MARKINGS

STRIP

FACING

ORGANZA

DOUBLE-STRIP

SLASH LINE

FACING

ORGANZA

BUTTONHOLES

FACING

WORKED BUTTONHOLE

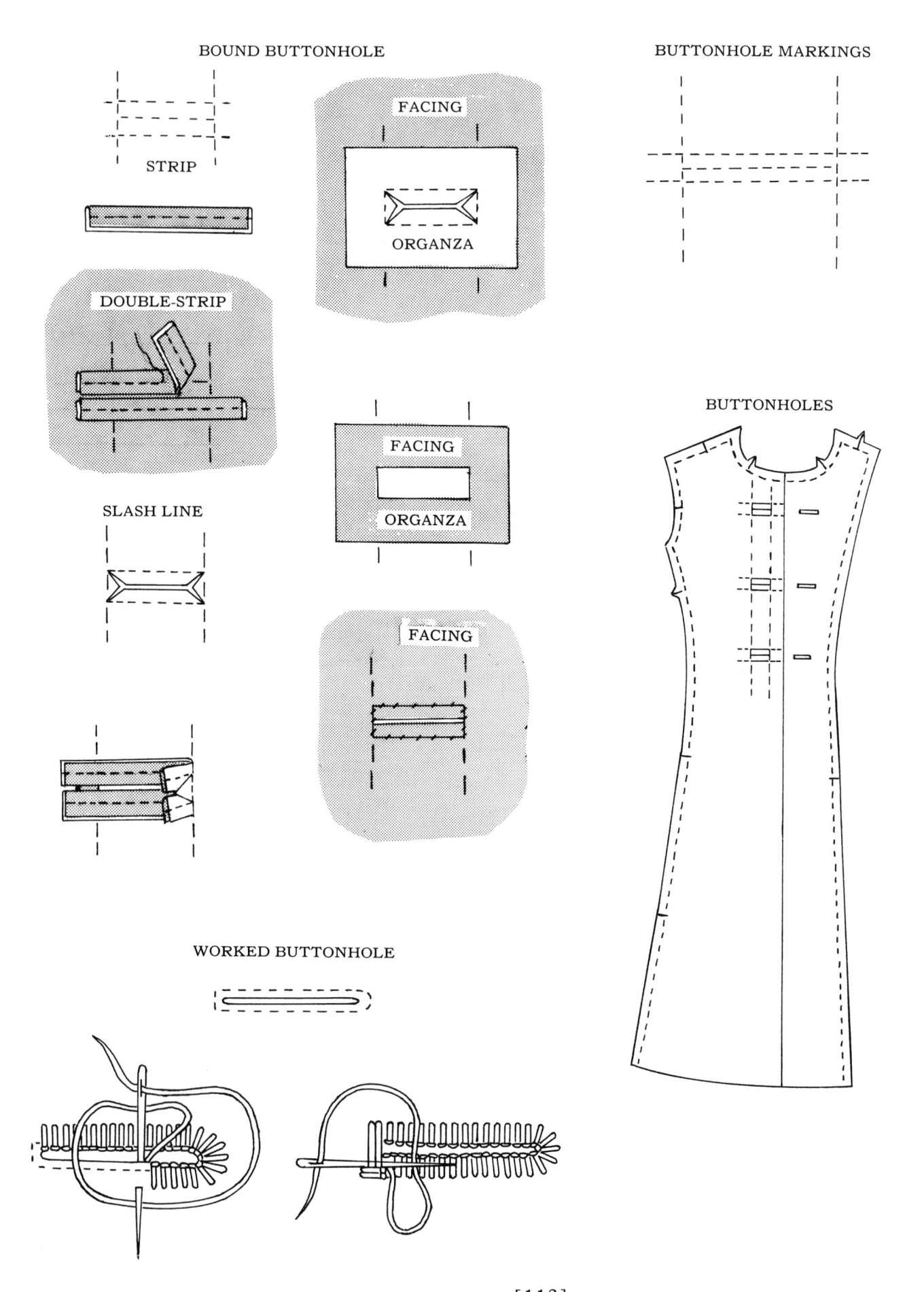

[113]

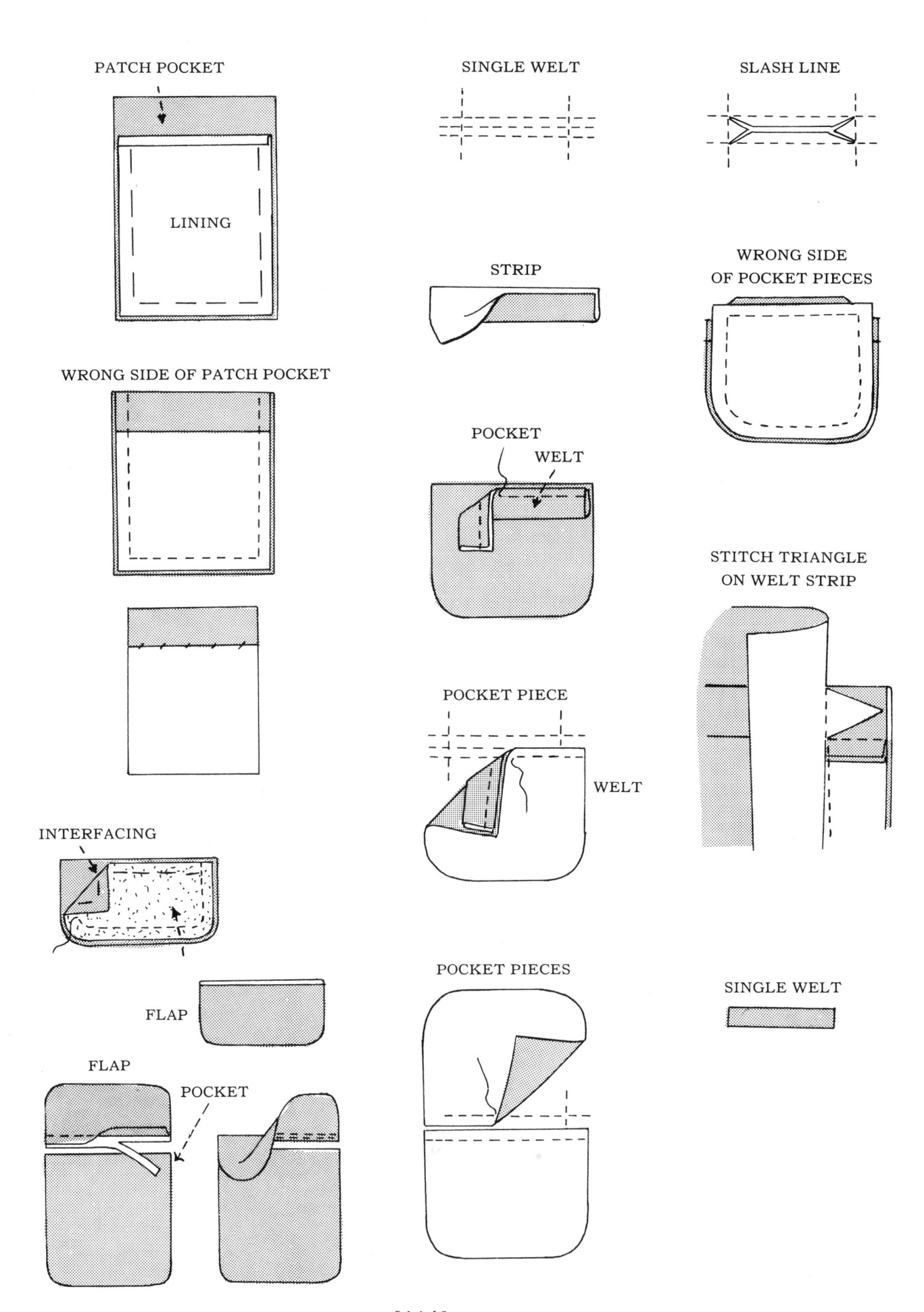

PATCH POCKET

LINING

SINGLE WELT

SLASH LINE

STRIP

WRONG SIDE
OF POCKET PIECES

WRONG SIDE OF PATCH POCKET

POCKET

WELT

STITCH TRIANGLE
ON WELT STRIP

INTERFACING

POCKET PIECE

WELT

FLAP

FLAP

POCKET

POCKET PIECES

SINGLE WELT

[114]

DOUBLE WELT

POCKET PIECES
ON DOUBLE WELT

SLANTED WELT

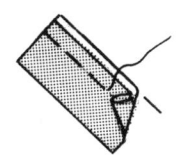

STRIP

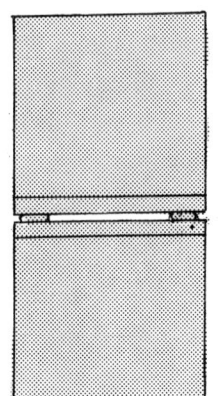

POCKET PIECE

WRONG SIDE
OF POCKET PIECES

DOUBLE WELT STRIPS

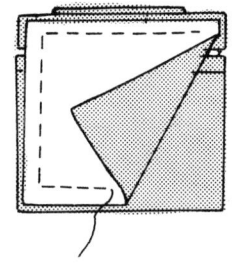

SLASH LINE

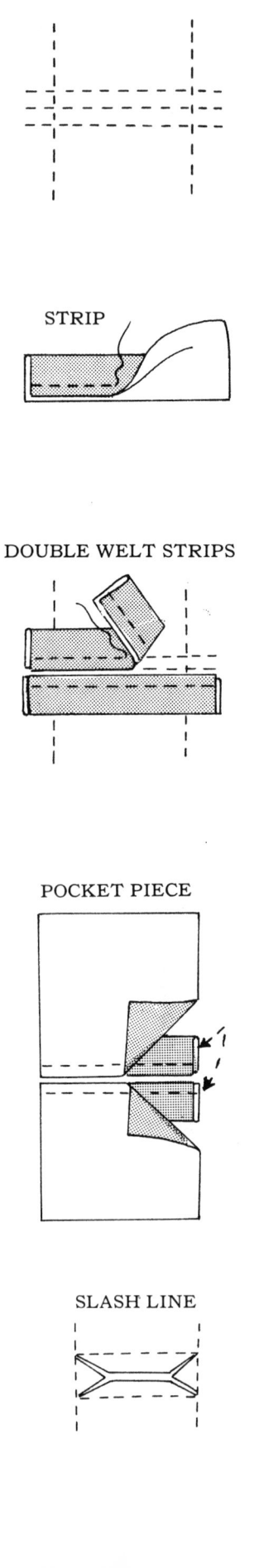

POCKET PIECE
THRU SLASH LINE

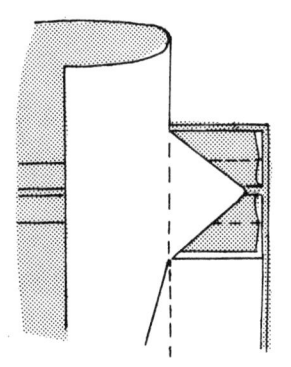

STITCHING TRIANGLE
ON DOUBLE WELT STRIPS

POCKET PIECE

POCKET PIECES

FRONT   BACK

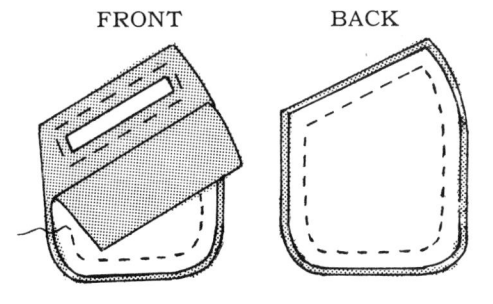

SLASH LINE

DOUBLE WELT

WELT

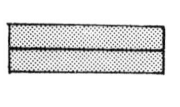

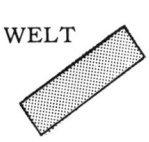

[115]

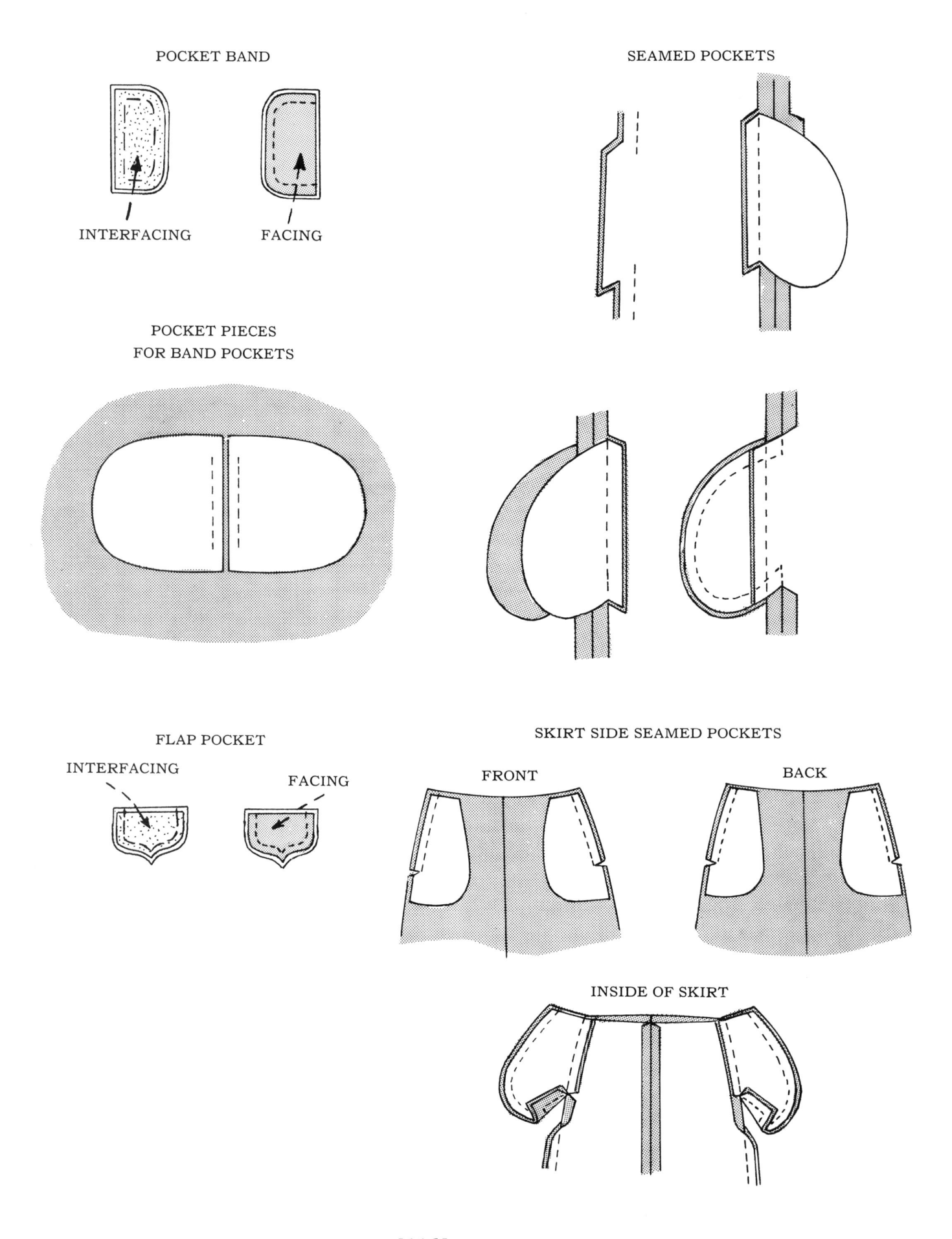

POCKET BAND

INTERFACING   FACING

SEAMED POCKETS

POCKET PIECES
FOR BAND POCKETS

FLAP POCKET

INTERFACING

FACING

SKIRT SIDE SEAMED POCKETS

FRONT   BACK

INSIDE OF SKIRT

[116]

COLLAR

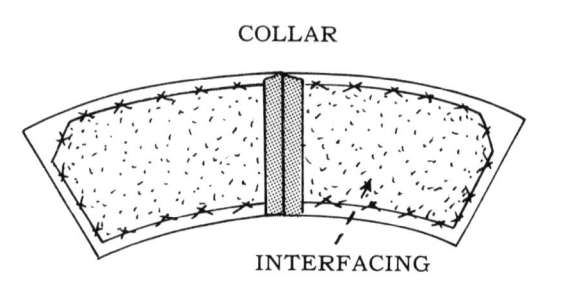

INTERFACING

BAND COLLAR

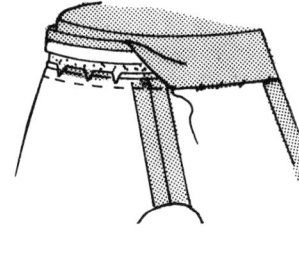

INTERFACING

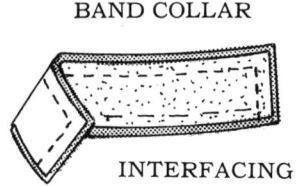

SHAPING COLLAR

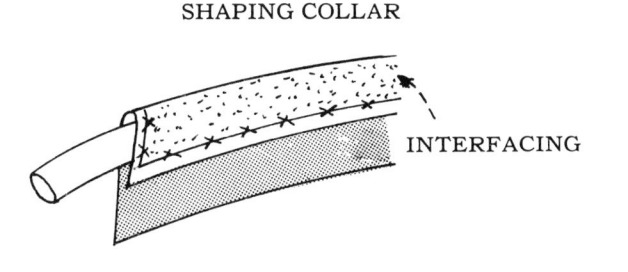

INTERFACING

MITRED BAND COLLAR

COLLAR

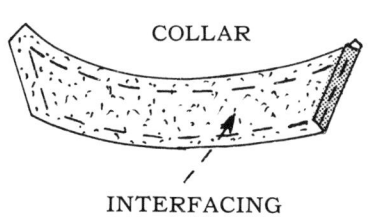

INTERFACING

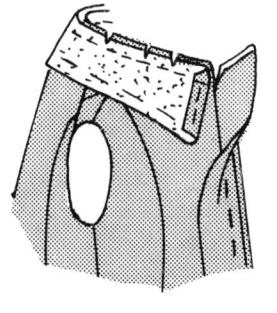

UNDER COLLAR

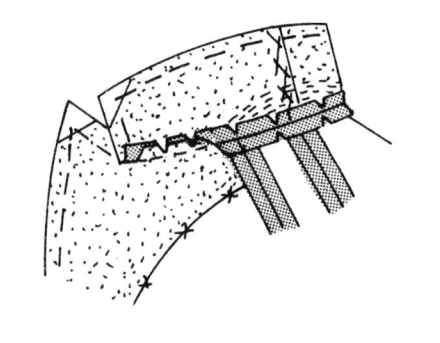

INTERFACING

JOINING FRONT FACING TO COLLAR

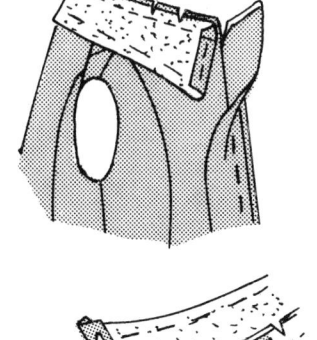

ATTACHING COLLAR
TO NECKLINE

NOTCH NECKLINE

FACING TURNED TO INSIDE

INTERFACING

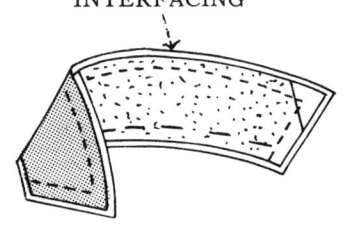

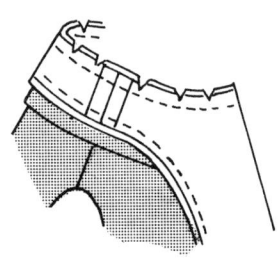

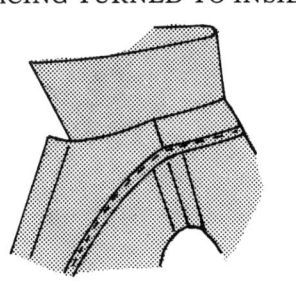

ATTACH COLLAR
STARTING CENTER BACK

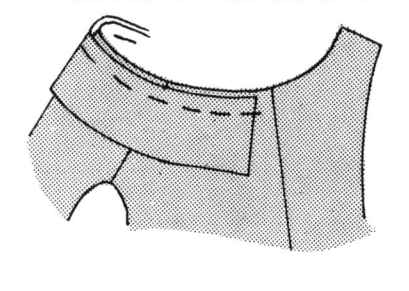

TURN FRONT FACING
OVER COLLAR

COLLAR   FACING

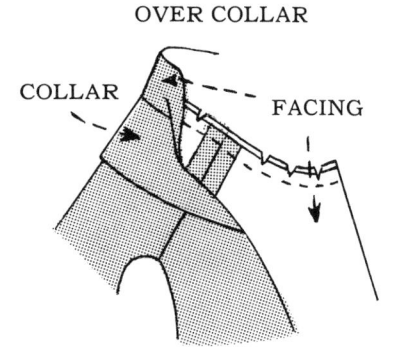

SHAPES OF INTERFACING
FOR
COATS OR JACKETS

INTERFACING

JOIN BACK AND
FRONT NECK FACING

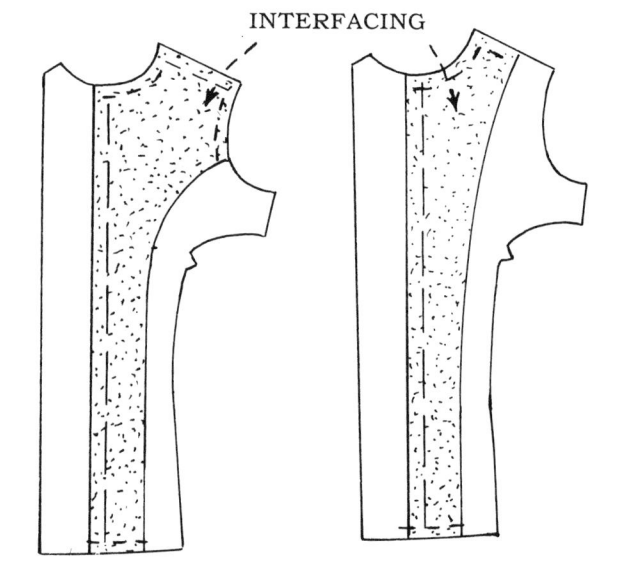

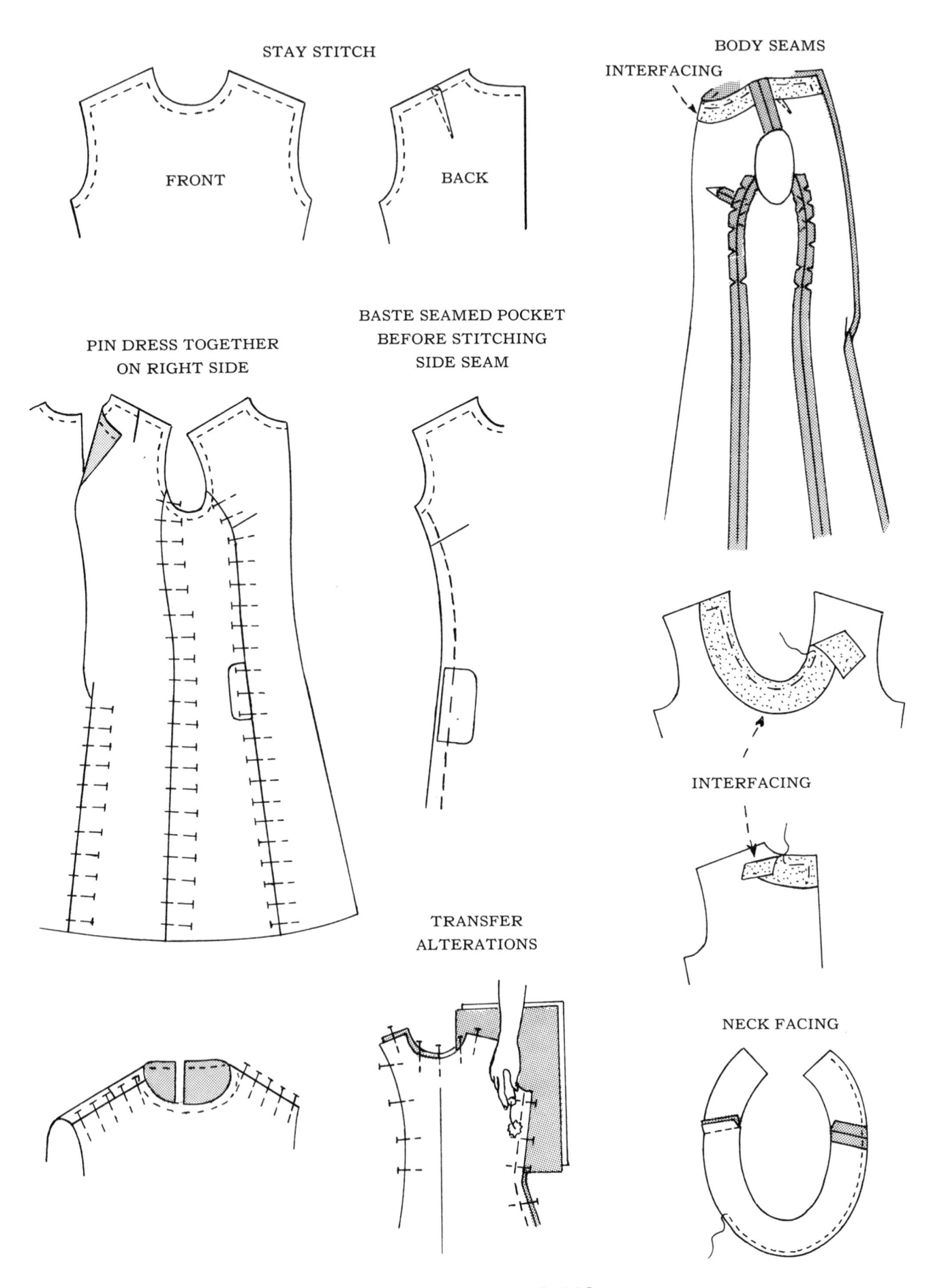

STAY STITCH

FRONT

BACK

BODY SEAMS

INTERFACING

PIN DRESS TOGETHER
ON RIGHT SIDE

BASTE SEAMED POCKET
BEFORE STITCHING
SIDE SEAM

INTERFACING

TRANSFER
ALTERATIONS

NECK FACING

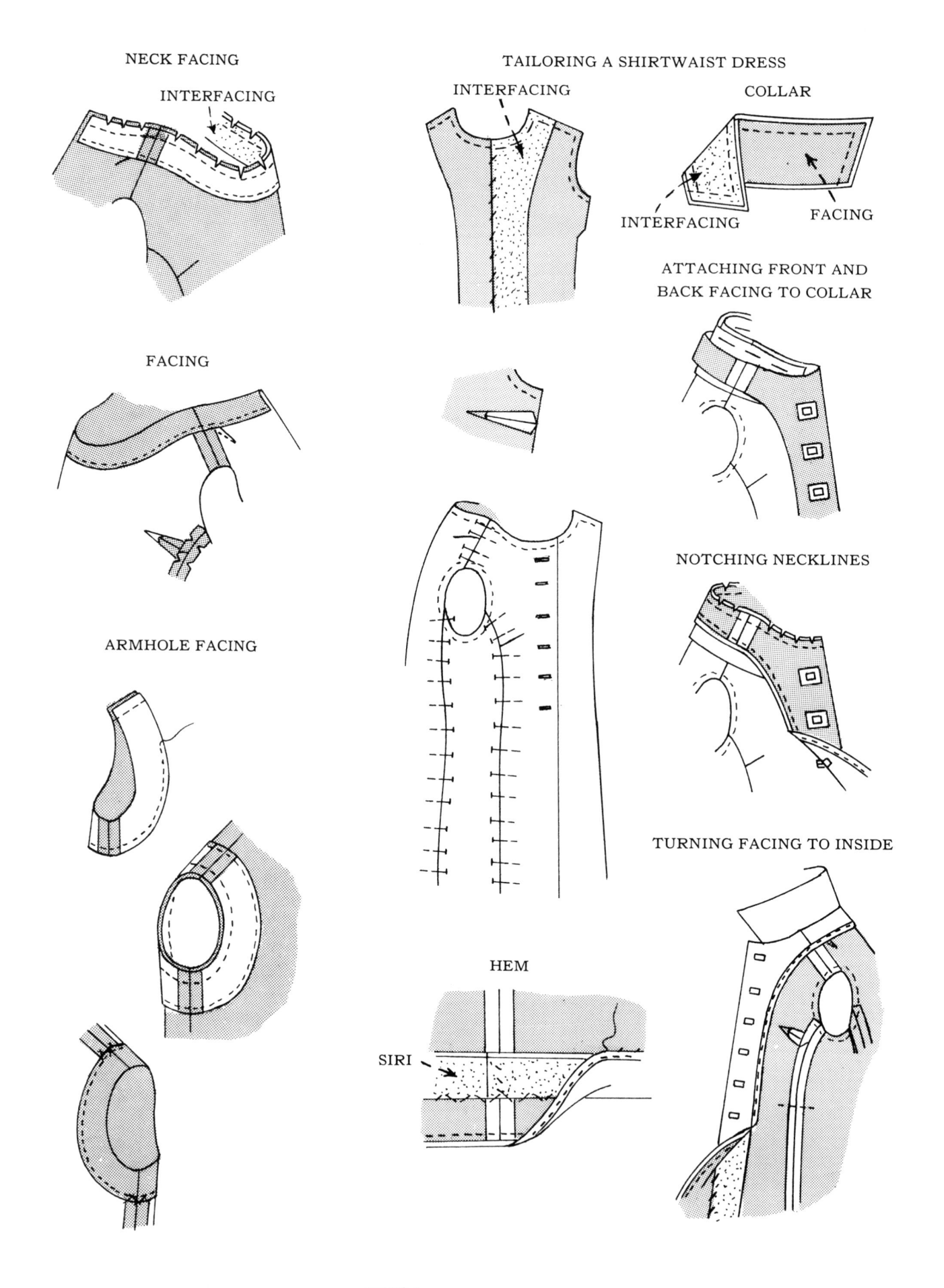

NECK FACING

INTERFACING

FACING

ARMHOLE FACING

TAILORING A SHIRTWAIST DRESS

INTERFACING

COLLAR

INTERFACING

FACING

ATTACHING FRONT AND
BACK FACING TO COLLAR

NOTCHING NECKLINES

TURNING FACING TO INSIDE

HEM

SIRI

STITCH SKIRT

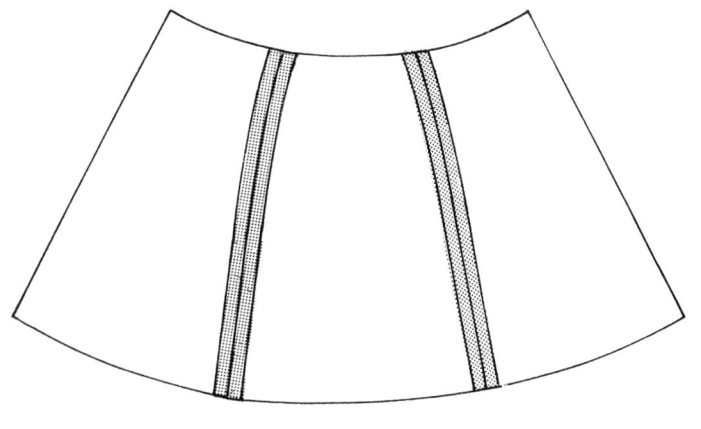

FOLD OF SIRI IN HEM

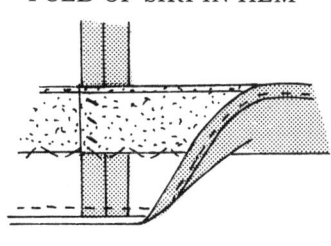

TURN UP HEM

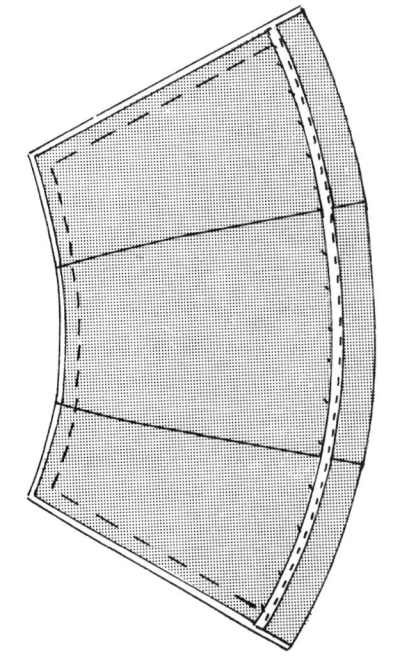

STITCH UNDERLINING

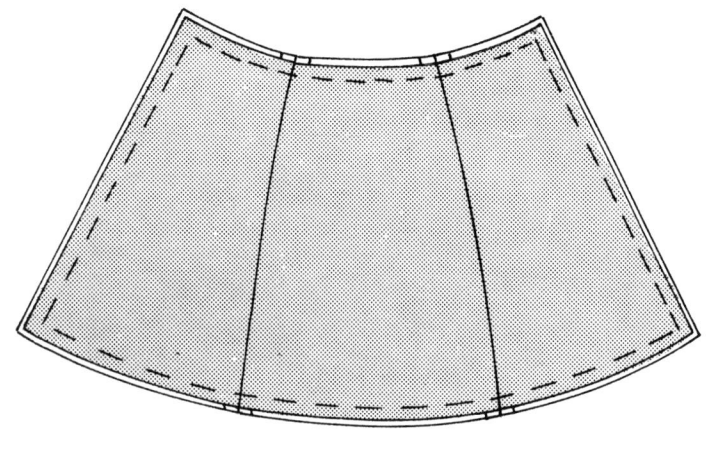

ATTACH UNDERLINING TO SKIRT
STITCHING ALL AROUND

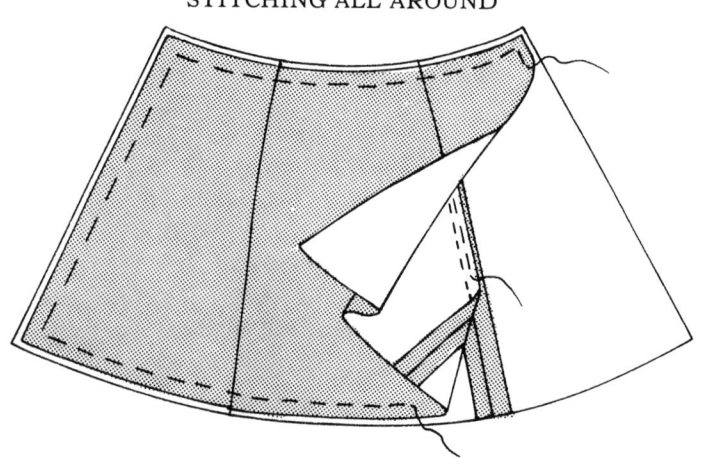

TURN BACK FACING

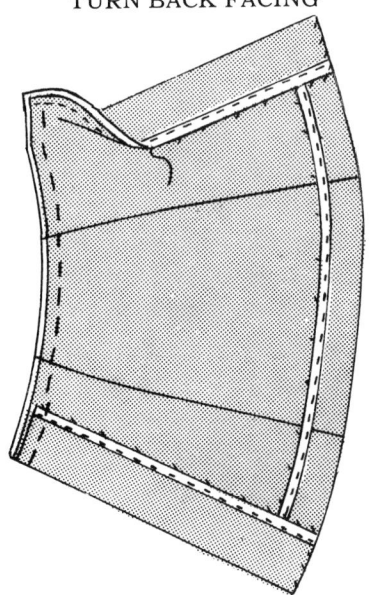

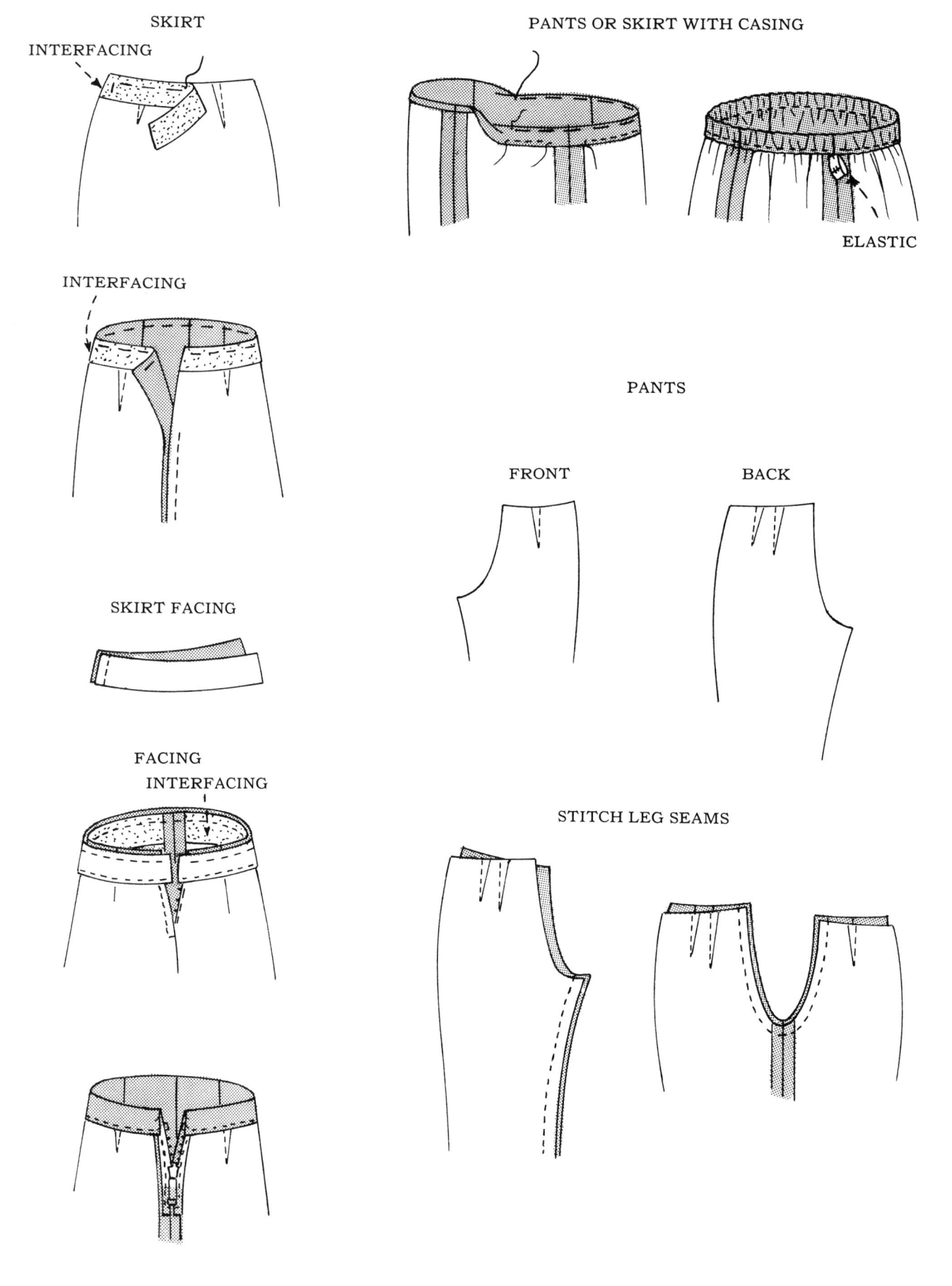

SKIRT

INTERFACING

PANTS OR SKIRT WITH CASING

ELASTIC

INTERFACING

PANTS

FRONT

BACK

SKIRT FACING

FACING
INTERFACING

STITCH LEG SEAMS

[122]

STITCH CROTCH SEAM

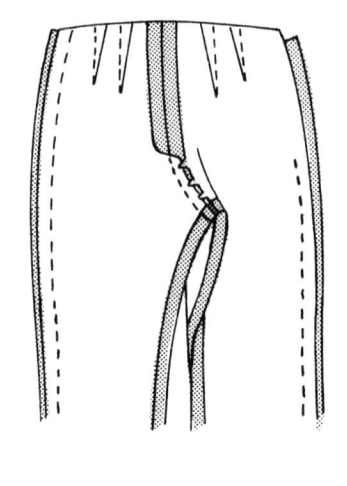

HEM FINISHES

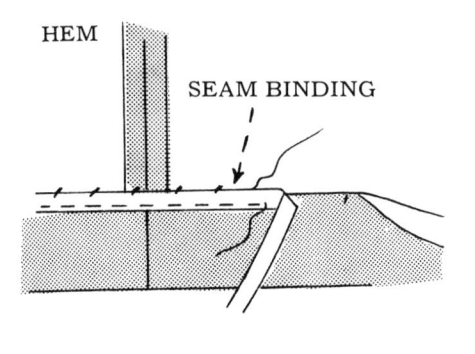

HEM

SEAM BINDING

WAISTBAND

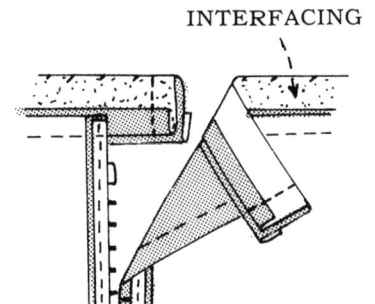

INTERFACING

DOUBLE STICH

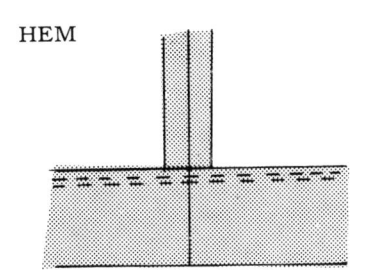

HEM

INTERFACING

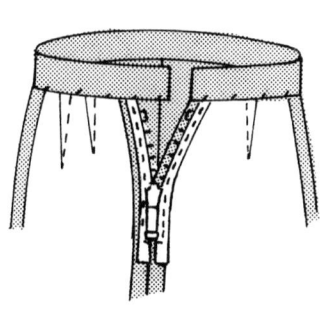

INTERFACING

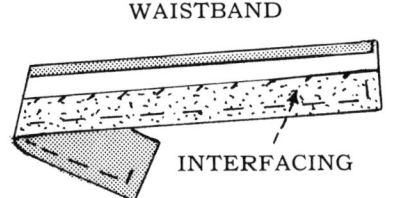

STITCH AND OVERCAST

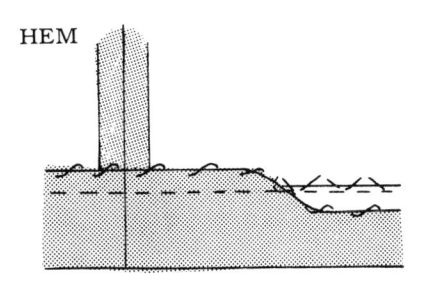

HEM

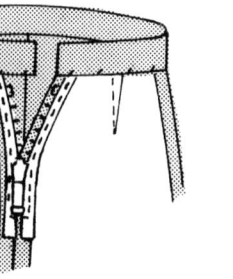

BLIND STITCH

HEM

[123]

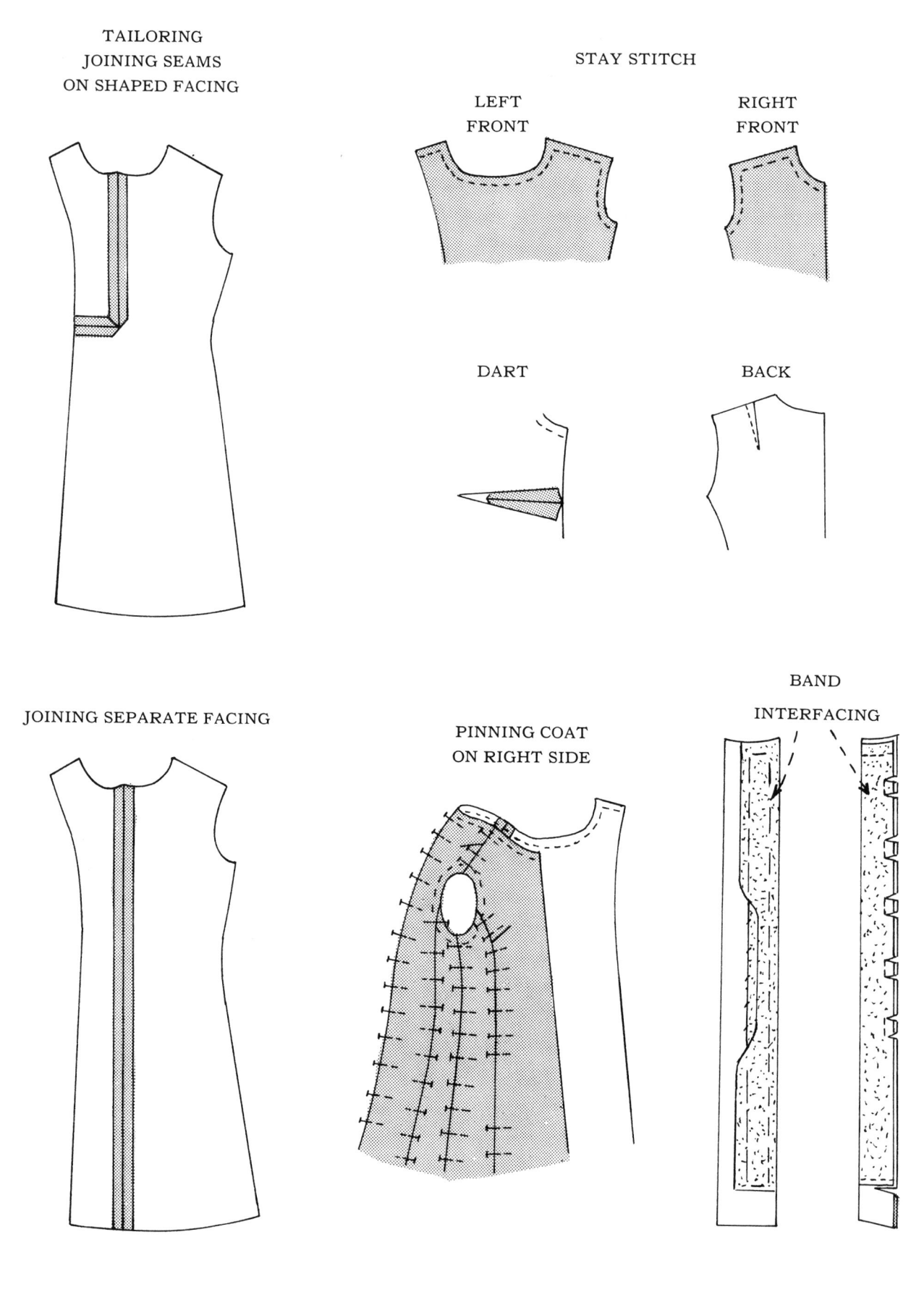

TAILORING
JOINING SEAMS
ON SHAPED FACING

STAY STITCH

LEFT
FRONT

RIGHT
FRONT

DART

BACK

JOINING SEPARATE FACING

PINNING COAT
ON RIGHT SIDE

BAND
INTERFACING

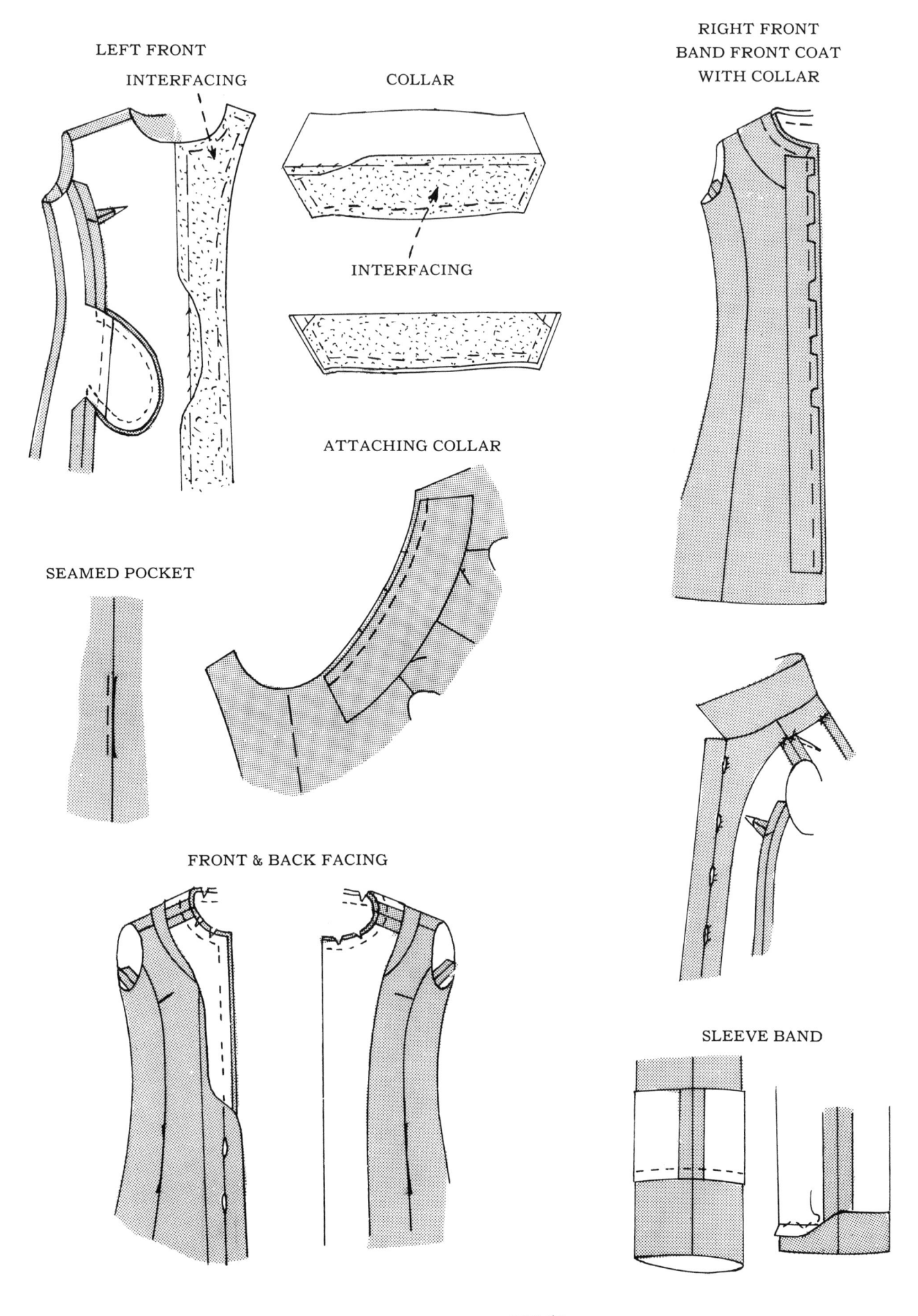

LEFT FRONT

INTERFACING

COLLAR

INTERFACING

RIGHT FRONT
BAND FRONT COAT
WITH COLLAR

ATTACHING COLLAR

SEAMED POCKET

FRONT & BACK FACING

SLEEVE BAND

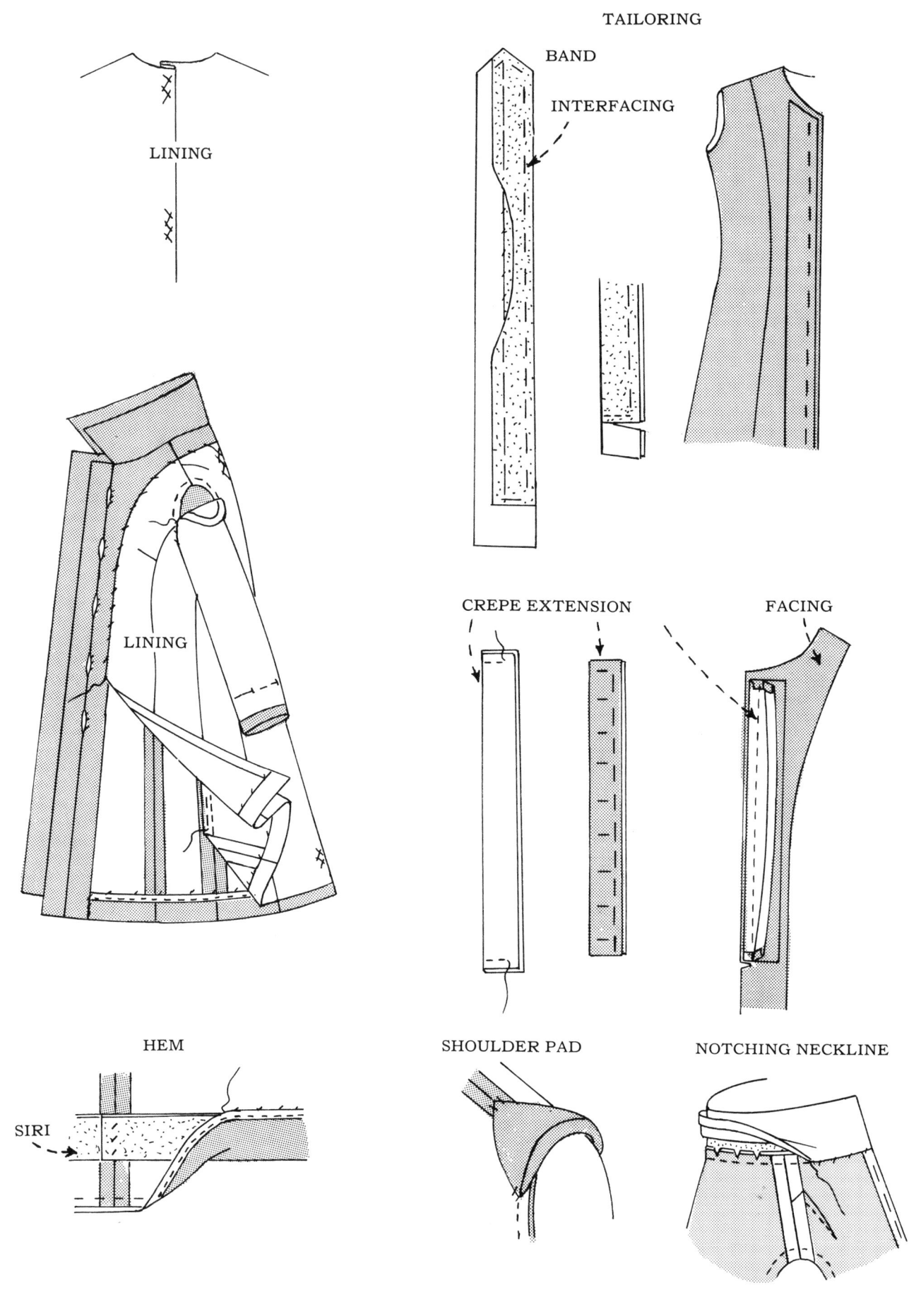

LINING

TAILORING

BAND

INTERFACING

LINING

CREPE EXTENSION

FACING

HEM

SIRI

SHOULDER PAD

NOTCHING NECKLINE

BAND FRONT COAT WITH BAND COLLAR

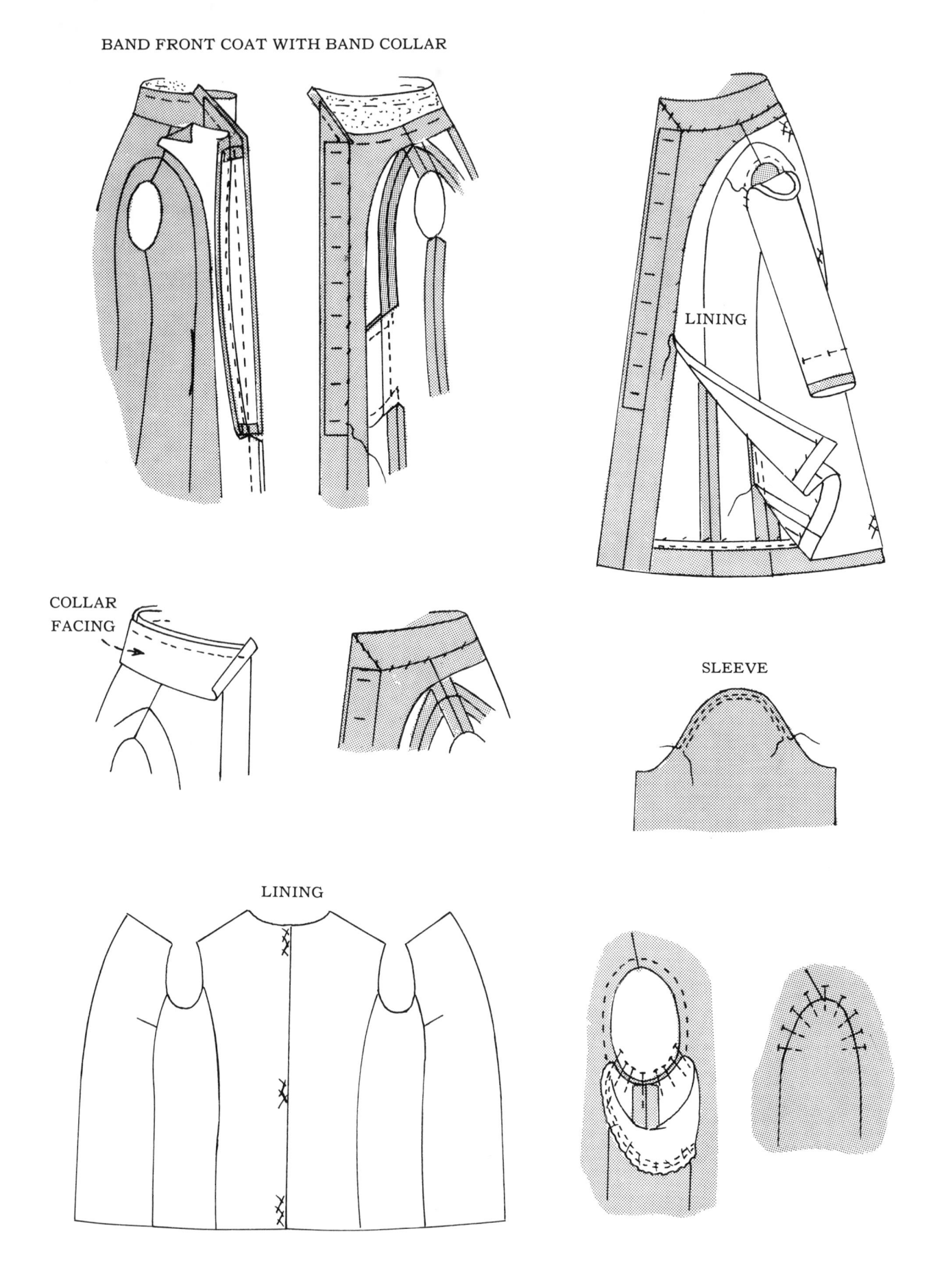

LINING

COLLAR
FACING

SLEEVE

LINING

MISCELLANEOUS

BELT

INTERFACING

INTERFACING

INTERFACING

CARDBOARD

LINING

GRADING SEAMS

TIE BELT

TABS

HEM

CORD

HOOK & EYE

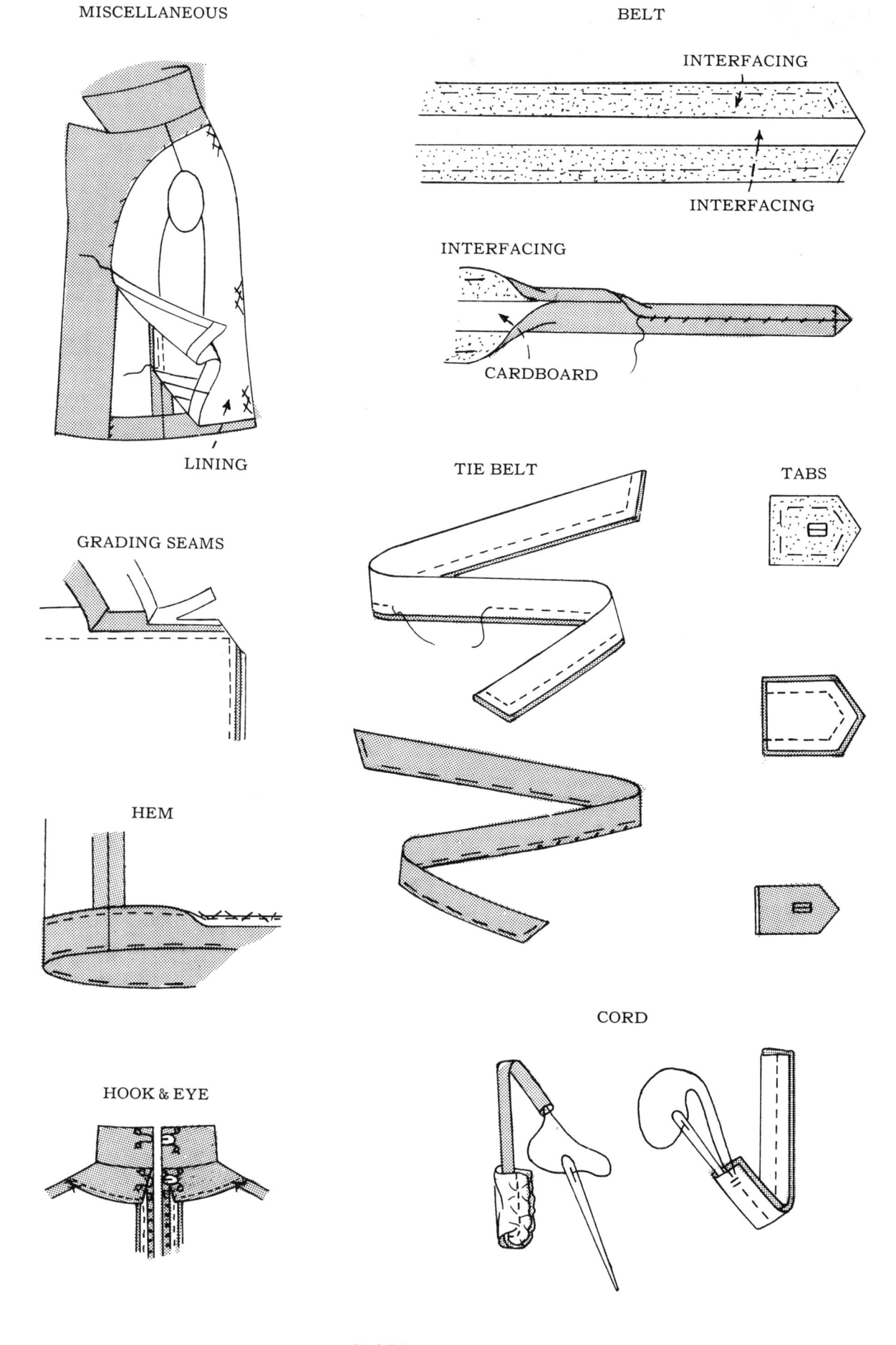

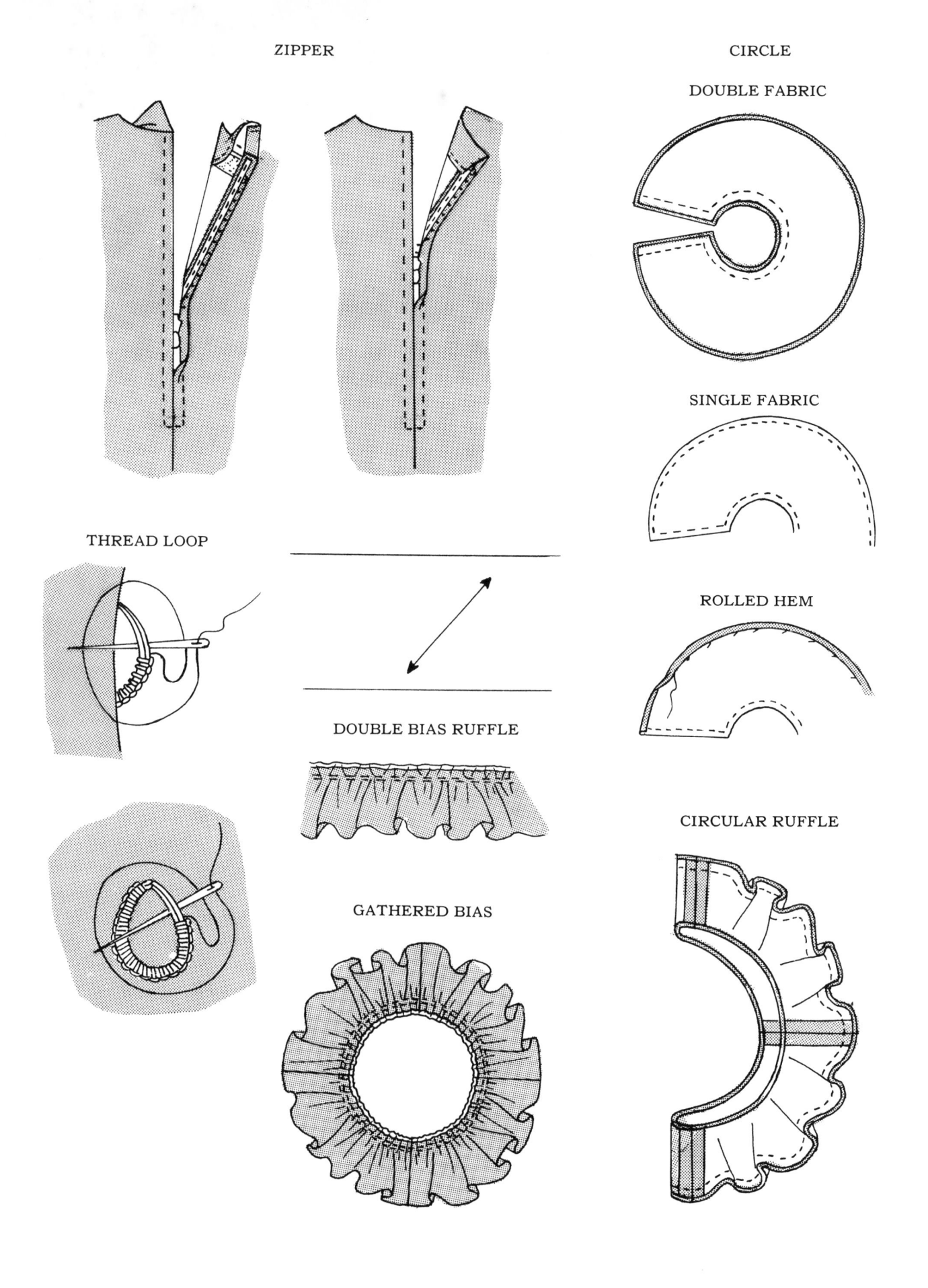

ZIPPER

CIRCLE

DOUBLE FABRIC

SINGLE FABRIC

ROLLED HEM

THREAD LOOP

DOUBLE BIAS RUFFLE

CIRCULAR RUFFLE

GATHERED BIAS

ABOUT THE AUTHOR

"One of the most rewarding art forms any woman can adopt is the full-fledged creation of a beautifully made, perfectly fitting and becoming wardrobe."

This sums up the philosophy of famous couturier Roxane, who developed a distinguished career as an award-winning designer. Happily, this talented fashion originator is now sharing her extensive fashion know-how with the woman who sews her own clothes. "To sew professionally, in the methods of *haute couture*, a woman needs techniques, tools, but above all—patience!" While she can't provide her readers with the latter, Roxane divulges all the "tricks of the trade" in her new book, *The Secret of Couture Sewing*.

Each chapter is heavily detailed and accompanied by how-to sketches; the subjects range from working with the proper equipment to the technicalities of tailoring a coat or suit.

For sixteen years Roxane designed a varied collection for one of Seventh Avenue's most prestigious manufacturers. Among her "firsts" were knit apparel from Italy, crocheted originals from Portugal, embroidered fashions from Madeira, Spain, and a group of English-made boutique-wear. She is the recipient of the industry's most coveted honors: the Coty Award and the International Silk Award, among many others.

For Roxane, fashion has been more than a career—it has meant the joy of creating something beautiful, the pride of accomplishment. [In her new book she provides readers with a vast body of fashion knowledge, enabling them to experience the same sense of joy and pride.]